Welcome to Texas

DRIVE FRIENDLY—THE TEXAS WAY

WELCOME
SPECIAL RANGER
Brownfield
Tahoka
Post
Seminole
Lamesa
Snyder
Andrews
Colorado City
Big Spring
Midland
Paso
Guadalupe Pk
8749
Guadalupe Mts
Del Rio

# ★ Texas
# BACK ROAD RESTAURANT
# Recipes

## A Cookbook & Restaurant Guide

### ANITA MUSGROVE

**Great American Publishers**
www.GreatAmericanPublishers.com
TOLL-FREE 1-888-854-5954

# Great American Publishers

171 Lone Pine Church Road • Lena, MS 39094
TOLL-FREE 1-888-854-5954 • www.GreatAmericanPublishers.com

ISBN 978-1-934817-25-4

by Anita Musgrove

Layout and design by Cyndi Clark

10 9 8 7 6 5 4 3 2 1

Every effort has been made to ensure the accuracy of the information provided in this book.
However, dates, times, and locations are subject to change.
Please call or visit websites for up-to-date information before traveling.

To purchase books in quantity for corporate use, incentives, or fundraising,
please call Great American Publishers at 888-854-5954.

# Contents

# Preface

## Are you ready for a new back road trip?

We have already traveled Alabama, Kentucky and Tennessee in the State Back Road Restaurant Recipes Cookbook Series. Now, let's crank up and take off for Texas, the Lone Star State. Each state has been an adventure and Texas is no exception. The second largest state in our United States, Texas is so large you can experience a diverse landscape with every direction you travel. It is, indeed, "Like a Whole Other Country." From coastal swamps and piney woods to rolling hills and rugged desert terrain to the mountains of Big Bend, come and experience it all as we travel back roads in search of the best locally-owned, Mom-and-Pop places to eat.

Author Anita Musgrove with husband Leonard, grandmother, and children, 1982, the year of the overnight Texas adventure.

My first trip to Texas was a whirlwind excursion with my husband, Leonard, and brother-in-law, Craig. We left about six in the evening, because Uncle John had died and Ethel Mae (my mother-in-law) needed her boys. You know when Mama calls, you go. We took off from Mississippi and got to Houston 12 hours later, driving mostly at night, arriving just in time to make Mama happy. I learned my first Texas lesson. You better know where you are going and what exit to take and be in the right lane at the right time, because traffic moves fast in Texas. After spending less than 24 hours in the Lone Star State, we were back on the road home.

NORTHWESTERN REGION

EASTERN REGION

SOUTHERN REGION

A couple of years, later Leonard woke me early one morning saying he would drive and I could sleep. We were on an adventure. I awoke a few hours later to discover that we were headed back to Texas, this time to Galveston. At least it was daytime for this trip, and I could see all that makes Texas special. It was everything I had always heard about... wide open spaces, long-horn cattle grazing along the way, blue bonnets growing on the side of the highways, and, when we got to Galveston, the beautiful coastline. Of course, we enjoyed dining at several great locally owned restaurants while we were there.

For our anniversary one year, our children, Sheila and Mickey, surprised us with a round trip visit to Texas, complete with a condo on the beach on South Padre Island and a car rental so we could explore. When it came time to eat, you guessed it, locally owned places are the best. On the Island one of the best places to eat is **Ted's Restaurant**. The favorite local item is the pecan pancakes, but with a huge menu, everyone can find something to satisfy their palate. If you don't see it on the menu, just ask Karen, and she will see about cooking it for you. If your trip is anything like mine, walking on the golden sands and watching spectacular sunsets will stay with you forever after visiting South Padre Island.

We have divided Texas into three regions to help you find your way to good eating. In the Northwestern Region you will find places like **New York Hill Restaurant** in Thurber where three generations of the Mills family will serve you the daily-made cinnamon rolls and yeast rolls along with the best steaks in the area. Enjoy the view atop New York Hill and the adjacent Thurber Historical Park. Be sure to also visit Kelli at **Valley Pecans** in Chillicothe. You will enjoy pecans grown right in their own orchards plus her "Dang Good Candy" made right on the premises.

While traveling through the Eastern Region, near Canton, be sure to stop at **Buttermilk's**. You'll take a step back in time when life was simple and food was created with passion to enjoy delicious dishes like chicken-fried steak and fried green tomatoes. Don't forget to stop at **J. Cody's** in Bryan and eat some mouth-watering barbecue and juicy rib-eye steaks cooked with mesquite wood over an open fire. When you stop, be sure to try the Cody Corn. Also, **John's Café** is a must stop. Mr. John has been in business 43 years serving the best buttery homemade biscuits for breakfast and hot roast beef plates for lunch. He still greets you as you enter through the doors. Say hi to his daughter, Georgia, for me.

Not to be out done by the other two regions the Southern Region holds its own place with good food. **Meyer's Elgin Smokehouse** in Elgin serves up food prepared with their family's heirloom recipes. Eat classic brisket and St. Louis-style ribs, slow smoked for 16 hours, along with eight varieties of smoked sausages. In Historic Fredericksburg, behind the ivy-covered walls of Cotton Gin Village, find Koi ponds with waterfalls, beautiful landscapes and **Cabernet Grill** which will entice you with a culinary experience you won't soon forget.

It takes a lot of people to publish a book like this, and we have a great team. First and foremost, I want to thank God for giving me the knowledge and strength to put these books together for you to enjoy. My appreciation and gratitude goes to my Texas partner, Tory Hackett. Thank you for helping make this book a reality. My heartfelt thanks go to Roger and Sheila Simmons who allow us to make these books the best they can be. Thank you both for the guidance and leadership that directs us the way we need to go. Brooke Craig, our Director of Operations, works with us every day to encourage us to do the best job possible. Thank you Diane Rothery, who makes sure the office runs smoothly, plus the rest of the Great American Team, Amber Feiock, Christi Griffin, Cyndi Clark, Gennell Goodman, Krista Griffin, Nichole Stewart, Pam Edwards, and Sheree Smith.

We have covered all of Texas in search of the best locally owned places to dine and compiled them here for your enjoyment. The book was made with a sense of adventure and a love of good food. It is my wish that you will discover a little piece of home as you enjoy reading about each restaurant, traveling to the establishments to enjoy the food they serve, and preparing their recipes at home for your family. Enjoy!

*Anita Musgrove*

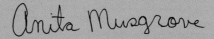

# Northwestern REGION

# Bogie's Downtown Deli

**241 Cypress Street • Abilene, TX 79601**

**325-672-3296**

**www.facebook.com/bogiesdeli**

Bogie's is known for outstanding sandwiches, salads, soups, and burgers named for movies of Hollywood's Golden Age. The movie memorabilia décor makes Bogie's a fun place for a casual lunch with friends. A trip anywhere near Abilene won't be complete without lunch at Bogie's. Catering for businesses and events is available, plus Bogie's offers a back room for groups.

**Monday – Friday: 10:30 am to 2:00 pm**

# The Cast of Bogie's Downtown Deli

*Dishes served in the restaurant are named after Humphrey Bogart movies. The year in parentheses is the year the movie came out (or, in the case of the Bogie's Hoagie, the year it was created—when Bogie's Deli opened).*

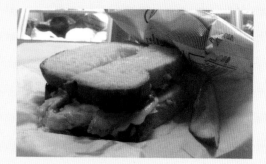

### The Oklahoma Kid (1939)

Set in the Southwest, the cast includes a succulent chicken breast, Monterey Jack cheese, a cameo appearance by avocado slices, and guest stars sourdough bread and Thousand Island dressing.

### The Barefoot Contessa (1954)

Starring roles by fresh-sliced mushrooms, avocados and purple onion topped with melted mozzarella on whole-wheat bread. Special cameo appearance by tomatoes, sprouts and Parmesan peppercorn dressing make this a performance not to be missed.

### Chain Lightning (1950)

This pleasantly shocking performance features roast beef with shredded Cheddar and Monterey Jack cheeses heated on a hoagie roll. Top it off with jalapeños and Parmesan peppercorn dressing and your taste buds will jump for joy.

### Bogie's Hoagie (1990)

A five-star performance by ham, Cotto salami, Genoa salami, provolone cheese and a hoagie roll. A special cameo by creamy Italian dressing, lettuce and tomato.

# Snack Shack

### 3201 North Highway 118
### Alpine, TX 79830
### 432-837-5699

Snack Shack is owned and operated by Paula Morehead ("Noni") and mother, Emily Scown ("Granny"). Food is prepared fresh with an extensive menu offering fajitas, burritos, nachos, burgers, salads, tacos, and sandwiches. Snack Shack is known for the famous, delicious "Texas Tater"—a baked potato with choice of barbecued brisket, sausage, or ham, and more than 12 different toppings. Try the "Shack Burger" with grilled onions, mushrooms, and Monterey Jack cheese, or the Texas-style smoked barbecued sandwich. They also make their own chili, serving it on Frito-chili pie, chili-cheese fries, and chili-on-a-bun. Their signature blended frozen drink—"Sno-ee's"—comes in a variety of flavors. Sweets include homemade cupcakes, and cookies.

**Monday – Saturday: 11:00 am to 7:00 pm**

## Queso Sausage Dog

### 1 (6-inch) German sausage link
### 2 (6-inch) hoagie rolls
### 1 (12-ounce) jar Monterey Jack queso (On the Border brand or similar)
### Jalapeños, chopped
### Cheddar cheese, shredded

Broil or grill sausage; cut in half lengthwise. Lightly toast hoagie rolls. Place a sausage on hoagie roll; top with warm queso. Garnish with chopped jalapeños and grated cheese. Add your favorite toppings.

### Restaurant Recipe

## Tex-Mex Dip

2 (9-ounce) cans bean dip

3 ripe avocados, mashed

½ cup mayonnaise

1 tablespoon lemon juice

1 (8-ounce) container sour cream

1 (1.25-ounce) package taco
seasoning mix

1½ cups shredded Cheddar cheese

4 green onions, finely chopped

1 small tomato, diced

Spread bean dip in bottom of a 12-inch round tray. In a large bowl, combine avocados, mayonnaise and lemon juice; spread over bean dip. In a separate bowl, combine sour cream and taco seasoning mix; spread over first 2 layers. Sprinkle with cheese, green onions and tomato. May be served immediately or cover loosely and refrigerate. Serve with tortilla chips.

**Local Favorite**

## Chocolate Cherry-Nut Cupcakes

1 box chocolate cake mix,
plus ingredients to prepare

2 (10-ounce) jars maraschino cherries,
drained, divided

1 cup chopped nuts, divided

2 (16-ounce) cans creamy
white frosting

1 (12-ounce) jar fudge ice cream
topping, heated

Preheat oven to 350°. Line muffin tins with paper bake cups; set aside. Prepare cake batter according to package directions. Chop 1 jar cherries; add to cake batter. Add ½ cup nuts. Spoon batter into prepared muffin cups, filling each about two-thirds full. Bake 16 to 20 minutes until done; cool 15 to 20 minutes. Pipe on frosting in a pastry bag fitted with a star tip. Drizzle with fudge. Sprinkle with remaining nuts. Place a cherry on top of each. Makes 24 cupcakes.

**Restaurant Recipe**

# The Big Texan Steak Ranch

**7701 I-40 • Amarillo, TX 79118**
**806-372-6000 • www.bigtexan.com**

Pair the biggest and the best food with a true western experience, and you get the world's most famous restaurant—The Big Texan Steak Ranch—a living legend. Founder R.J. "Bob" Lee grew up on the lore of the Old West. When he went looking for a good steak, served with Texas flair, and failed to find one, he turned his disappointment into determination, and dreams into reality. The Big Texan Steak Ranch opened on Old Route 66 in 1960. The story of the FREE 72-ounce steak is legendary. Regulars, cowboys from working ranches, turned good natured bragging into a contest, and the winner consumed 4½ pounds of steak, a baked potato, salad, shrimp cocktail, and dinner roll. The original meal and rules are still in place: Complete it in one hour; don't leave the table until you're finished; and, if you lose your dinner, you lose the contest. Today, The Big Texan Steak Ranch sprawls alongside Interstate 40, featuring a motel with a Texas-shaped swimming pool, horse hotel, gift shop, candy store, and micro-brewery.

**365 days a year: 8:30 am to 10:30 pm**

## Roquefort Dressing

**6 gallons Kraft mayonnaise**

**1 cup lemon juice**

**5 ounces MSG**

**1 gallon whole milk**

**¼ cup salt**

**¼ cup white pepper**

**3 pounds (½ wheel) Roquefort cheese, crumbled**

**10 pounds blue cheese, crumbled**

**1 ounce egg-shade food coloring**

Combine mayonnaise, lemon juice, MSG, milk, salt and pepper; mix well until smooth. Add cheeses and mix slowly to retain chunks. Add in the egg color last and gently stir well. Cover, label with time and date, store in cooler until needed. Makes 8½ gallons. Keeps 4 days in cooler.

**Restaurant Recipe**

# Potager Café

**208 South Mesquite Street**
**Arlington, TX 76010**
**682-553-5811**
**www.potagercafe.com**
**www.facebook.com/potagercafe**
**potagertexas@gmail.com**

Most restaurants just don't get it right, feeding you way too much food prepared in industrial kitchens; or if they do use ingredients from local farms, you need your rent money to pay the bill. Potager Café is different. They really do know the farmers and ranchers where they get most of their ingredients, they make everything from scratch, and they serve you only as much as you know you can eat (food is way too precious to waste). And then they trust you to pay a fair price for it. Yes, they don't give you a bill, because they know you are honest and appreciate good food like your Ol' Granny used to make for you.

**Tuesday & Wednesday:**
**11:00 am to 3:00 pm**
**Thursday – Saturday: 11:00 am to 9:00 pm**

## Potager Quiche

PAUL KNUDSEN

*Many people are afraid of making pastry. But pastry is probably the easiest thing in the world to make, as long as you remember a few things: keep it cold, do it fast and don't overwork your dough— which is why it is fast and easy. This recipe makes enough pastry for 2 tarts. Use one and freeze the other. When you are ready to use it, let it thaw in the refrigerator overnight and you will have a fast, easy, delicious dinner in about half an hour.*

### Pâte Brisée (Pastry Crust):

**2 cups organic all-purpose flour**
**Good pinch of salt**
**½ cup (1 stick) very cold, unsalted organic butter, cut into half-inch cubes**
**1 egg, beaten**
**½ cup ice water**

Pulse flour and salt in the food processor about 10 times to distribute salt evenly. Add cold butter, and process just long enough to look like crumbly sand (counting to 12 is just about right). Don't overprocess, or dough will be tough. You don't want the flour to absorb the butter, so be sure to keep it cold...which means work fast (especially here in Texas). In a cup, lightly beat egg and water, then toss in with flour mixture. Process a few seconds, until it comes together in a nice ball. I let it do 3 revolutions around the bin, and boom, it's done. (Remember, don't overprocess it. )

Now comes a fun part...Julia Child called it "The Big Smear." Turn dough out onto a smooth surface (granite works wonderfully), and, again working quickly, start smearing lumps of dough about the size of a small egg, out along the surface, to blend ingredients nicely. This is very different from kneading dough; don't do that. Smear one lump, then another, and keep going until it's all smeared and piled up into a heap. Gather it up, divide into 2 pieces, and form into disks. Wrap in plastic wrap and refrigerate at least 1 hour (overnight is best).

Generously flour a smooth rolling surface. Unwrap rested disk of dough, sprinkle with flour and start smacking it with your rolling pin, to soften it up enough to roll out. Once it starts to get pliable, start rolling it, picking up and turning it about a quarter turn every roll or two. Always roll in just one direction—out. Don't roll back and forth, which makes dough tough. Make sure surface is always well floured, so dough doesn't stick. Roll out into a circle, about an inch and a half bigger than tart tin. (I like tart tins with a removable bottoms.) Drape dough over

rolling pin, and transfer to tin. Gently ease it into pan, fitting it into bottom. You will have about half an inch or so of dough extending from the top of tart tin. Fold that over like a hem, and press it to the sides, to reinforce them (this will make it stronger to hold ingredients). Prick pastry all over with a fork.

*Quiche Filling:*

**Enough chopped, cooked vegetables to cover bottom of tart**

**Chunks of whatever cheese you find tasty**

**3 eggs, beaten**

**Salt and pepper to taste**

**½ cup organic whole milk**

**½ cup organic heavy whipping cream**

Preheat oven to 375°. Scatter vegetables over bottom of pastry crust. We've put just about every vegetable (even okra!) into our quiche and it's all delicious. May also use meat such as bacon, ham or salmon. Distribute cheese evenly on top. Beat eggs lightly with a pinch of salt and a few grinds of fresh pepper. Add milk and whipping cream. Beat just until blended; don't overbeat. Pour over vegetables and cheese, and pop into oven. Bake about 30 minutes, or until set and top is golden brown. Let rest 5 minutes, or it will be too gooey to cut.

**Restaurant Recipe**

# Sugar Creek Grill

**304 East 2nd Street**
**Big Lake, TX 76932**
**325-884-1500**
**Find us on Facebook**

Sugar Creek Grill is located in the heart of oilfield country in west Texas. Sugar Creek brings a unique twist to west Texas cuisine. With a diverse menu featuring a little bit of everything from burgers, pastas, Tex-Mex, and to their ever-popular hand-cut steaks, you are sure to find a dish to please you. Sugar Creek strives to be the best. The food's so great you will scrape your plate.

**Monday – Friday: 11:00 am to 9:00 pm**

## Mashed Potatoes

**4 medium potatoes, peeled and cut in cubes**

**5 tablespoons butter**

**½ cup half-and-half**

**¼ teaspoon salt**

**Dash black pepper**

In a saucepan, cover potatoes with water. Bring to a boil over high heat. Reduce heat to low; simmer 15 minutes or until potatoes are tender. Drain. Add butter and milk; mash until smooth.

**Local Favorite**

## Chicken–Fried Steak

**1½ cups whole milk**

**2 large eggs**

**2 cups all-purpose flour**

**2 teaspoons seasoned salt**

**1½ teaspoons black pepper**

**¾ teaspoon paprika**

**¼ teaspoon cayenne pepper**

**3 pounds cube steak**

**½ cup vegetable oil**

**1 tablespoon butter**

Mix milk with the eggs; pour into shallow dish. In another shallow dish, mix flour, salt and seasonings. Coat meat with dry mixture, then in wet mixture and again in dry mixture. Place on wire rack until ready to fry. Heat oil in large skillet over medium heat. Add butter; place steak in skillet to fry until golden brown both sides. Save drippings for gravy.

*Gravy:*

**⅓ cup all-purpose flour**

**½ teaspoon seasoned salt**

**Black pepper, to taste**

**3 to 4 cups whole milk**

Add flour to pan drippings; whisk until golden brown. Add salt and pepper; stir to mix. Add milk, stirring constantly until smooth and thick. Serve over steak and mashed potatoes.

**Local Favorite**

# Valley Pecans

**1001 Highway 287
Chillicothe, TX 79225
940-852-5957 • 877-268-8488
www.valleypecans.com**

Valley Pecans owners Mike and Kelli Baustert, who live in the middle of the pecan orchards, started out by selling pecans in red mesh bags out of the back of their pick-up. When they sold out, that was it for the year. Today they have 2 buildings not only housing the best pecans you have ever eaten, but Kelli, with her keen sense for decorating, also offers a really eclectic blend of items for sale along with "Dang Good Candy," including a wide variety of food items and Texas-inspired gifts—even Horny Toad replicas, always a favorite—but don't forget the pecans.

**Monday – Saturday: 8:30 am to 5:30 pm
Sunday: 10:30 am to 5:30 pm
Deli Hours: Monday – Saturday: 11:00 am to 3:00 pm**

## Pecan Nuggets

*Make on dry days only.*

**4½ cups chopped pecans**

**1¾ cups brown sugar**

**1 cup flaked coconut**

**1 teaspoon salt**

**2 tablespoons honey**

**4 egg whites**

**½ teaspoon vanilla**

Mix pecans, brown sugar, coconut, salt, honey, egg whites and vanilla. Mix by hand till ingredients hold together. Line sheet pan with foil or parchment paper. Drop by teaspoons 1 inch apart. Bake at 350° for 18 minutes.

**Restaurant Recipe**

## Pecan Pie

**3 eggs**

**½ cup evaporated milk (or heavy cream)**

**½ cup corn syrup**

**1 cup sugar**

**2 tablespoons butter, melted**

**1 teaspoon vanilla**

**⅛ teaspoon salt**

**1½ cups coarsely chopped pecans**

**½ cup pecan meal**

**1 teaspoon vinegar**

**1 (9-inch) unbaked pie shell**

Beat eggs well and stir in remaining ingredients, except pie shell. Pour into unbaked pie shell. Bake at 325° for about 1 hour and 10 minutes or until crust is brown and filling is slightly puffy.

**Restaurant Recipe**

# Owl Drug Store
## Old-Fashioned Soda Fountain & Grill

**312 Commercial Avenue • Coleman, TX 76834**
**325-625-2178 • Find us on Facebook: Owl Drug**

Imagine yourself escaping the big city blues. Whether you hail from Dallas, Austin, or San Antonio, getting off the beaten path and taking the back roads to Owl Drug will take you back to a real "Texas Mayberry" experience where you have to try really hard not to engage in friendly conversation about Coleman Bluecat Football, hunting, or family in this setting where everyone seems remarkably familiar. The Owl Burgers are fresh, malts and milkshakes are made to order, and the onion rings are made right before your eyes. It is well worth a 20-minute detour.

**Monday – Friday: 8:00 am to 5:00 pm**
**Saturday: 8:00 am to 2:00 pm**

## Famous Owl Drug Chocolate Banana Milkshake

**2 heaping scoops chocolate Blue Bell ice cream**

**¼ cup milk**

**½ banana**

**Whipped cream**

**1 cherry**

In blender, add ice cream, milk and banana. Process until smooth and pour into a serving glass. Serve with whipped cream and a cherry on top.

**Restaurant Recipe**

## Owl Drug Buttermilk Pie

**1½ cups sugar**

**3 eggs**

**½ cup butter**

**½ cup buttermilk**

**Pinch salt**

**2 tablespoons flour**

**1 teaspoon vanilla**

**Unbaked pie shell**

Mix all ingredients together, except pie shell. Pour into pie shell. Bake at 325° for 1 hour.

**Restaurant Recipe**

## Owl Drug World Famous Piggy Burger

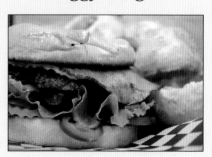

**2 premium ground beef patties**

**2 slices American cheese**

**1 hamburger bun, toasted**

**Lettuce leaf**

**Onion slice**

**Tomato slice**

**Dill pickle slices**

**Pickled jalapeño slices**

**1 strip bacon, fried and cut in half**

**1 ham slice, grilled**

Place patties on hot grill. Cook first side 5 minutes; flip and cook second side 3 minutes. One minute before patties are done, lay one slice cheese on each patty; allow to melt. On bottom bun, lay lettuce, onion, tomato, dill pickles and jalapeños. Place one patty on bottom bun; add bacon. On bun top place second patty, and ham. Close sandwich.

**Restaurant Recipe**

# Star Beau's

**134 West Central • Comanche, TX 76442 • 325-356-2869**

Star Beau's is located on the southwest corner of the historic Comanche square. The restaurant is located on the bottom floor of an 1890 bank building that still maintains its original exterior. Beau Blackwell and his sidekick, Lammy Morrison, have been serving up delicious, fresh foods for 20 years. The menu features sandwiches, salads, pastas, burgers, steaks, fried foods, and signature meringue pies, made daily by Mom, Janetta Blackwell.

**Monday – Saturday:
10:30 am to 9:00 pm**

## Chocolate Crème Pie

### Filling:

1½ cups sugar, divided

2 tablespoons flour

2 tablespoons cornstarch

2 tablespoons cocoa

2 cups milk

3 egg yolks (save whites for meringue)

¼ cup butter, melted

1 teaspoon vanilla extract

1 (10-inch) pie shell, baked

Sift sugar, flour, cornstarch and cocoa together; mix well. Whisk egg yolks and milk together; strain into dry ingredients. Whisk in butter. Microwave 3 times for 3 to 4 minutes, whisking after each until mixture is thick but pourable. Whisk in vanilla and pour into pie shell.

### Meringue:

¾ cup water

¼ cup sugar

1 tablespoon cornstarch

3 egg whites

1 teaspoon vanilla extract

¼ teaspoon cream of tarter

In saucepan over medium heat, combine water, sugar and cornstarch. Heat until syrup forms. Beat egg whites, vanilla and cream of tarter until opaque. Combine with syrup and beat until fluffy. Spread over Filling, and bake at 375° for 10 to 12 minutes or until lightly browned.

**Restaurant Recipe**

## Star Beau's Chicken Salad

8 cups chopped, boiled or baked chicken breasts

3 cups finely chopped celery

1 cup finely chopped red onion

3 cups mayonnaise (good quality)

1½ tablespoons dried Italian seasoning blend

2 teaspoons salt

1 teaspoon pepper

Shred chicken in food processor. Combine with remaining ingredients and mix well. Makes about 3 quarts. Recipe can easily by halved or doubled.

**Restaurant Recipe**

# BBQ on the Brazos

**9001 Highway 377**
**Cresson, TX 76035**
**817-396-4758**
**www.bbqonthebrazos.com**

Owned & Operated By
An Old West Texas Racer
And A South Texas Cowgirl

BBQ on the Brazos' company philosophy is quite simple: "We blow smoke, one piece of hardwood at a time. The 'ART' of Texas barbecuing is mastering the indirect heat method of smoking meats, and we have done that through many years of experience. We use only the best raw products money can buy, the freshest ingredients, and hand-selected hardwoods to produce our finished products. We stand behind the fact that our smoked meats will create a memory—one bite at a time." Happy trails from BBQ on the Brazos.

**Monday – Friday: 6:30 am to 3:00 pm**
**Saturday: 9:00 am to 3:00 pm**

## Fresh Ground Brazos Brisket Burger

1 pound flat-cut beef brisket, trimmed
and cut into 1-inch pieces

2 tablespoons olive oil

¼ teaspoon kosher salt

⅛ teaspoon fresh-ground black pepper

4 Cheddar cheese slices

4 jalapeño cheese sourdough buns

Chipotle mayonnaise

4 tomato slices

4 green lettuce leaves

Cut and layer brisket on baking pan. Freeze 15 minutes or until meat is firm, not frozen. Combine meat and olive oil in a large bowl. Put meat thru grinder completely. Put meat thru grinder a second time. Divide mixture into 4 equal parts. Shape into ½-inch-thick patties. Press indention in middle of each patty. Preheat grill to medium-high heat. Sprinkle patties with salt and pepper. Place on grill rack coated with cooking spray. Grill 3 minutes, or until grill marks show. Carefully turn patties over and grill 3 more minutes. Place cheese on top and grill until desired doneness. Toast buns and coat with chipotle mayonnaise. Top each with a slice of tomato and a lettuce leaf.

**Restaurant Recipe**

## Brazos Steak Sandwich

6 thin slices skirt steak, fat trimmed

Worcestershire sauce

Tony Chachere's Creole seasoning
to taste

2 eggs, beaten

1 cup milk

1 avocado, peeled and sliced

Panko breadcrumbs

1 yellow onion, sliced

½ cup salsa

1 tablespoon canola oil

Jalapeño cheese sourdough buns

Dredge steak in Worcestershire sauce then sprinkle with Creole seasoning; set aside. Combine egg and milk; beat well. Dip avocado slices in egg/milk mixture then panko breadcrumbs. Fry in hot oil until crispy; set aside. Grill 3 minutes on each side over hot grill until medium rare. Slice into strips. Place sliced onion in skillet with salsa and oil; sauté until tender. Grill buns. Layer with fried avocados, sliced meat, sautéed onion and salsa.

**Restaurant Recipe**

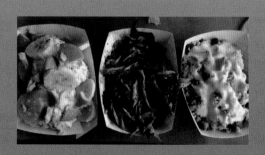

# Tater's Café

**111 South 1st Street**
**Crowell, TX 79227**
**940-684-1491**
**www.taterscafe.com**
**www.facebook.com/Taters.Cafe**

Tater's Café's delicious menu is inspired by the everyday family cooking of times past. You'll feel at home while enjoying a great meal in the casual and relaxed dining area. Experience the home-cooked meals, attentive service, and a friendly, hometown atmosphere. Come see what makes Tater's one of the most popular cafés in town. Tater's has been in business since December 2008.

**Monday – Saturday:**
**6:00 am to 2:00 pm**

**Sunday:**
**8:00 am to 2:00 pm**

## Brown Sugar Pecan Bars

¼ cup butter, melted

1 cup packed brown sugar

1 egg, beaten

¾ cup all-purpose flour

1 teaspoon baking powder

½ teaspoon vanilla extract

¾ cup chopped pecans

Preheat oven 350°. Spray or lightly grease an 8-inch pan. Add brown sugar to melted butter and stir until smooth. Stir in beaten egg. In a separate bowl, stir together dry ingredients until mixed. Once mixed, stir dry ingredients into brown sugar and butter mixture. Add vanilla and pecans; mix. Pour into pan and bake 20 minutes.

**Restaurant Recipe**

## Yummy Potatoes

3 pounds baking potatoes

1 stick margarine, melted

4 green onions, chopped (green parts)

⅓ cup soy sauce

1 tablespoon Worcestershire sauce

½ pound bacon, cooked and crumbled

Salt and pepper to taste

Wash potatoes well (do not peel). Cut in quarters and cook in water to cover until done; drain. Put in a broiler pan. Melt butter; add onions, soy sauce and Worcestershire. Pour over potatoes and sprinkle with bacon and salt and pepper. Broil just until potatoes are brown on top, about 5 minutes.

**Local Favorite**

## Creamy Lemon Pie

1 (8-inch) pie crust, baked

3 egg yolks

1 (14-ounce) can sweetened condensed milk

½ cup lemon juice

2 drops yellow food coloring

1 (16-ounce) carton Cool Whip

Preheat oven to 325°. Beat eggs yolks with condensed milk and lemon juice. Stir in food coloring. Pour into pie shell; bake 30 minutes. Cool. Refrigerate; serve topped with Cool Whip.

**Local Favorite**

# TC's Ponderosa
### MESQUITE SMOKED
## BAR-B-Q

**136 West US Highway 82**
**Dickens, TX 79229**
**806-623-5260**
**Find us on Facebook: TCs Ponderosa**

*"Just east of Lubbock and off the West Texas Caprock is some of the most flavorful barbeque that has ever graced a red & white checked tablecloth."* —*Taste* magazine

Truck drivers, travelers, and locals love to pick up the specialty smoked meats at the deli that is conveniently located on USA Highway 82 in Dickens, Texas. Tom Hale is very particular about smoking the meats using mesquite wood that he personally cuts and cures for several weeks. The store is famous for its chopped beef sandwich using only lean brisket. Other smoked meats include ham, black peppered turkey, German sausage, sliced brisket, and hot links. Sides include red beans, cowboy coleslaw, and Mrs. Hale's pineapple pudding for desert. Expect to be treated like family when you walk up to order and sit down to eat.

**Monday – Thursday: 7:00 am to 8:00 pm**
**Friday: 7:00 am to 9:00 pm**
**Saturday: 8:00 am to 9:00 pm**
**Sunday: 8:00 am to 8:00 pm**

## Cowboy Coleslaw

4 cups chopped green cabbage

2 cups chopped purple cabbage

2 carrots, shredded

½ onion, chopped

1 (15-ounce) can whole-kernel corn, drained

2 tablespoons diced pimentos

1 cup chopped green bell pepper

*Dressing:*

1 cup white or cider vinegar

½ cup sugar

¼ cup water

6 tablespoons olive oil

1 teaspoon dry mustard

½ teaspoon cayenne pepper

1 teaspoon onion powder

1 teaspoon celery seed

1 tablespoon dry ranch dressing mix

½ teaspoon salt

½ teaspoon black pepper

Combine vegetables; add dressing. Mix well and serve.

**Restaurant Recipe**

## Pineapple Pudding

1 cup dry instant vanilla pudding mix

2 cups milk

1 cup pineapple juice

1 (14-ounce) can sweetened condensed milk

2 (8-ounce) cans pineapple tidbits, drained

1 (16-ounce) carton Cool Whip

Vanilla wafers for topping (optional)

Combine pudding mix, milk and pineapple juice; beat about 2 minutes. Stir in condensed milk and pineapple tidbits. Fold in Cool Whip. Top with whole or crushed vanilla wafers, if desired.

**Restaurant Recipe**

# Circle M Bar-B-Q
# and Texas Grill

**9003 Interstate 20 Access Road**
**Eastland, TX 76448**
**254-631-0058**
**www.steakhouseeastland.com/bbq**

This is casual Texas dining at its best, with a comfortable family atmosphere and a courteous friendly staff to serve you. Since 1982, John has been cooking brisket and catering to the public. The moist, tender, and savory brisket is the best around, and Circle M is also well known for grilled rib-eye steaks. Other local favorites include ribs, sausage, and pulled pork, as well as burgers, chicken, fried okra, and fries. Their chicken-fried steak is the best. Save room for dessert—homemade cobblers topped with ice cream. Come for the outstanding food, and the staff and prices will keep you coming back for more.

**Tuesday – Saturday: 11:00 am to 9:00 pm**
**Sunday: 11:00 am to 2:00 pm**

## Pork Shoulder

### Pork Rub:

**2 cups brown sugar**

**1½ teaspoons red pepper**

**3 tablespoons paprika**

**1 tablespoon cumin**

**1 tablespoon black pepper**

**1 tablespoon garlic powder**

**1 tablespoon onion powder**

**2 tablespoons salt**

Combine all ingredients. Store in an airtight container. Makes enough for 3 pork shoulders.

### Pork Shoulder:

**1 (5-pound) bone-in pork shoulder**

Rub a third of pork rub over shoulder. Place shoulder fat-side-up in a smoker heated with hickory or pecan wood. Smoke at 225° for 6 hours. Remove from smoker and wrap in foil. Cook another 4 to 5 hours, until meats starts to fall apart.

**Restaurant Recipe**

## Grandmother's Blackberry Cobbler

**2 quarts blackberries**

**2 cups sugar plus more for sprinkling on top**

**3 heaping tablespoons cornstarch**

**2 cups all-purpose flour**

**1 teaspoon salt**

**⅔ cup shortening**

**5 to 6 tablespoons cold water**

**½ cup butter, melted**

Add blackberries, 2 cups sugar and cornstarch to a saucepan; bring to a boil. Simmer 15 minutes; set aside to cool. Mix flour and salt in bowl; cut in shortening. When it looks like crumbles, add water a spoonful at a time. Mix just until smooth. Divide crust into 2 balls. Roll out into shape of pan, pressing one crust into bottom. Add blackberry mixture. Place other crust over top. Brush with butter; poke 6 to 8 holes in top crust. Sprinkle with sugar. Bake at 350° for 1 hour or until golden brown.

**Family Favorite**

# Fort Davis Drugstore and Hotel

**111 State Street
Fort Davis, TX 79734
432-426-3118
www.fortdavisdrugstore.net**

Since 1913, Fort Davis Drugstore has been a gathering spot for locals. In 1950, it was relocated across the street to the building it resides in today, and in the early 1980s hotel space was added. When you visit this unique business, you will enjoy great food —breakfast, lunch, and dinner—or may cool off with an ice cold pop from the old-fashioned soda fountain. After you dine in, stick around and visit the Art Gallery upstairs, and even spend the night in one of six uniquely decorated rooms. Have a sweet tooth? Fort Davis Drugstore offers an array of candies, homemade butter cream fudge, and homemade pies. The choices are endless. While you're there, be sure to visit the gift shop filled with shirts, mugs, and more. Whatever you do, don't miss stopping at Fort Davis Drugstore and Hotel, where you will have an experience you won't soon forget.

**Daily: 7:00 am to 9:00 pm**

## Drugstore Green Chile Cheeseburger

½ pound hand-patted 81/19 ground beef

Montreal Beef Seasoning to taste

1 large hamburger bun

1 whole (canned) green chile

2 slices Swiss cheese

1 leaf lettuce

1 slice tomato

4 pickle slices

1 slice onion

Make sure edges of patty are sealed and grill over medium heat. Lightly season one side with Montreal Beef Seasoning. Butter bun and grill. Split green chile in half lengthwise and lightly grill. Just before burger is ready to remove from grill, place green chile on bun, add 2 slices Swiss cheese and steam with a "squirt" of water at edge of burger to melt cheese. Serve hot with standard burger toppings and a side of chips for a really great southwestern treat.

**Restaurant Recipe**

## Quick Chipotle Sauce

*This Quick Chipotle Sauce has a great shelf life and really spices up a burger.*

1 (12-ounce) can chipotle peppers in adobo sauce

1 cup ranch salad dressing

Purée all ingredients in food processor. Refrigerate until ready to use.

**Restaurant Recipe**

## My Mama's Cobbler

1 stick butter

1 cup all-purpose flour

1 cup sugar

2 teaspoons baking powder

½ teaspoon salt

1 cup water

1 teaspoon Mexican vanilla

Canned fruit of your choice: peaches, plums, apples or sweetened berries

2 tablespoons brown sugar

1 teaspoon cinnamon

Melt butter in a 9x13-inch glass baking pan. Lightly mix dry ingredients with water and vanilla. Pour batter over hot melted butter. Top with canned fruit. Sprinkle with brown sugar and cinnamon. Bake at 350° until topping is golden brown. Serve with ice cream while it's hot out of the oven.

**Family Recipe**

# B's Family Dining

**101 North Main Street**
**Fort Stockton, TX 70735**
**432-336-8499**
**Find us on Facebook: B's Family Dining**

In the heart of historic Fort Stockton, you'll find a little gem known as B's Family Dining. Originally opened in 1927 as a pharmacy and soda shop, it is also known as Bulldog Corner from the group of gentlemen that love to come "shoot the bull." September 2012, the restaurant was purchased by the Shuttleworths and after a year of renovating, the doors were opened to serve the first buffet consisting of homemade Old-Fashioned Meatloaf and B's Chicken-n-Dumplin's. A lunch buffet is served weekdays along with menu items such as the Signature Burger and Steak Fries.

**Monday & Tuesday: 11:00 am to 6:00 pm**
**Wednesday – Friday: 11:00 am to 8:00 pm**
**Buffet: 11:00 am to 2:30 pm**
**STEAK NIGHTS:**
**Wednesday – Friday: 4:30 pm to 7:30 pm**

# B's Chicken-n-Dumplin's

### Chicken:

**2 (5-pound) roasting chickens**
**Olive oil**
**Butter, softened**
**Salt and pepper to taste**

Split chickens, skin-side-up, and rub with olive oil and butter. Season with salt and pepper. Roast in 375° oven for 45 minutes. Cool, remove skin and shred meat. Save the juices.

### Stock:

**3 gallons chicken stock
(homemade is preferred)**
**3 yellow onions, diced**
**3 carrots, grated**
**3 stalks celery, diced**
**3 tablespoons chicken bouillon**
**2 teaspoons granulated garlic**
**1 tablespoon poultry seasoning**
**Salt and pepper to taste**

Place all stock ingredients in a large pot over medium-high heat. Cook until veggies are tender. Add saved juices from roasted chicken. Add a few drops of yellow food coloring for a more pleasing presentation. Keep at a boil while making dumplings.

### Dumplings:

**4 cups all-purpose flour**
**1 teaspoon baking powder**
**1 teaspoon salt**
**1 teaspoons pepper**
**1 stick butter**
**1 tablespoon dried parsley flakes**
**2 eggs**
**Buttermilk**
**2 tablespoons flour**
**1 cup milk**

In a large bowl, combine flour, baking powder, salt and pepper. Cut in butter and parsley flakes and mix to fine crumbles. Add eggs and enough buttermilk to make a nice dough. Drop tablespoon-size balls of dough into boiling stock, reduce heat to simmer. Cover and cook until dumplings are cooked through. Remove dumplings to a bowl and set aside. Add shredded chicken. Stir flour into milk until all lumps disappear. Add to liquid to thicken. Return dumplings to pot and serve hot.

**Restaurant Recipe**

# Kincaid's Hamburgers

## www.kincaidshamburgers.com

Kincaid's opened in 1946 as a neighborhood specialty grocery store priding itself on its butcher shop. The butcher, O.R. Gentry, individually custom cut fresh meat for his customers daily. To ensure his freshly ground chuck didn't go to waste, he began cooking hamburgers on a small griddle in the store. His goal was to keep it simple, but strive to make the perfect burger. Chasing perfection finally paid off in 1983 when Kincaid's was awarded "The Best Hamburger in America." Today the Gentry family continues to rack up awards and provide their loyal customers with the perfect burger.

**Monday – Saturday:**
11:00 am to 8:00 pm

**Sunday:**
11:00 am to 3:00 pm

**6 LOCATIONS:**

**4901 Camp Bowie**
**Fort Worth, TX 76107**
**317-732-2881**

**4825 Overton Ridge Blvd.**
**Fort Worth, TX 76132**
**817-370-6400**

**3124 Texas Sage Trail**
**Fort Worth, TX 76177**
**817-750-3200**

**100 North Kimball Avenue**
**Southlake, TX 76092**
**817-416-2573**

**3900 Arlington Highlands**
**Boulevard #113**
**Arlington, TX 76018**
**817-466-4211**

**220 Adams Drive**
**Weatherford, TX 76086**
**817-594-7773**

## Real Texas Chili

*Make one to two days before serving for best results. Never add beans to a Texan's chili! We tend to be stubborn about this and believe us, you do not want to hear it.*

**2½ pounds ground beef**

**1 tablespoon dried minced onion**

**1 cup beef broth**

**1 cup chicken broth**

**1 (12-ounce) bottle dark beer**

**1 (8-ounce) can tomato sauce**

**2 teaspoons beef bouillon**

**1 teaspoon chicken bouillon**

**1 teaspoon cayenne, divided**

**3 tablespoons dark chili powder**

**2 serrano peppers, pierced with a fork**

**2 jalapeños, pierced with a fork**

**¼ teaspoon black pepper**

**¼ teaspoon white pepper**

**2 teaspoons garlic powder**

**3 tablespoons light chili powder**

**1½ tablespoons ground cumin**

**¼ teaspoon kosher salt**

**Shredded Cheddar cheese (optional)**

**Chopped onions (optional)**

Cook ground beef in a pan over medium heat with minced onion until grayed and fully cooked. Drain off all fat. Put meat in a stockpot; add broths, beer and tomato sauce. Bring to a boil; reduce heat to low. Add beef and chicken bouillon, ½ teaspoon cayenne, dark chili powder and serrano and jalapeño peppers; simmer for 1 hour, stirring occasionally. While pot is simmering, get out 2 bowls. In the 1st bowl, add black pepper, white pepper, garlic powder and light chili powder. This is your 1st dump. In the second bowl, add ½ teaspoon cayenne, cumin and salt. This is your 2nd dump. When your pot has finished simmering for an hour, dump the 1st bowl in the pot; continue simmering for 30 minutes, stirring occasionally. Add the 2nd dump; simmer for at least 15 minutes. Note that the longer the chili simmers the thicker and more developed it becomes. Discard the serrano and jalapeño peppers before serving. Top with cheese and onions and serve with sweet cornbread or saltines. Serves 5 to 6.

**Restaurant Recipe**

# TRAILS INN RESTAURANT

**3007 East Highway 82**
**Gainesville, TX 76240**
**940-668-8325**
**www.facebook.com/Trails-Inn-Restaurant**

Trails Inn is a family-owned, Mom and Pop style café where all the locals enjoy eating. The guys like to come hang out, drink coffee, and shoot the breeze. Located just outside of town proper within the city limits where the old High Ho Drive-In Theatre was located, Trails Inn enjoys serving many wonderful people, including visitors from afar plus all their regular travelers that keep coming back for more of the food they have learned to love. Grady says, "I wish to thank all of our customers for the many years of dining and friendship."

**Sunday – Thursday: 6:00 am to 2:00 pm**
**Friday & Saturday: 6:00 am to 8:00 pm**

## Meatloaf

**10 pounds ground chuck**
**2 tablespoons salt**
**2 tablespoons black pepper**
**1 tablespoon garlic powder**
**1 medium white onion, chopped**
**1 green bell pepper, chopped**
**10 to 12 large eggs**
**1 cup Heinz 57 Sauce**
**1 (16-ounce) can diced tomatoes**
**1 (16-ounce) can tomato sauce**
**4 cups crushed crackers**

In an extra large mixing bowl, mix together meat, salt, pepper, garlic powder, onion and bell pepper. While wearing gloves, mix ingredients into meat with your fingers. Add eggs, Heinz 57, diced tomatoes and tomato sauce; mix well by hand. Add crackers and mix. Divide into 8 to 10 loaves; bake 3 hours in a preheated 425° oven. Serves 35 to 40 people.

**Restaurant Recipe**

## Stewed Cabbage

**2 to 3 heads green cabbage**
**1 stick butter**
**1 tablespoon salt**

Tear apart cabbage and remove stem. Fill an extra large pot with 10 cups water. Put cabbage in water with butter and salt. Cook over medium heat, bringing to a boil. Boil about 10 minutes, stirring occasionally. Drain and put in steam tray until ready to serve. Serves 30.

**Restaurant Recipe**

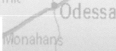

## The Grille at the Harbor on Possum Kingdom Lake

**1693 Park Road 36
Graford, TX 76449
940-779-7600
www.harborliving.com
thegrill@harborliving.com**

Newly renovated, The Grille boasts spectacular lakeside outdoor dining. This fine, yet casual, restaurant is right on the lake. With the warmth of a county lodge, it features an all-day menu of fine American cuisine with an extensive wine and beverage list. The Grille offers Texas-style dining with a southwestern flair. Ten convenient courtesy slips allow you to boat up to the restaurant and walk right in. Dine on the patio or patio bar for lunch or dinner, and watch the boats go by, or choose to enjoy a sumptuous dinner beneath a canopy of stars. The choice is yours at The Grille at the Harbor.

**Monday – Sunday Corporate Retreats (Located in Our West Wing Facilities)
Thursday – Saturday: 11:00 am to 10:00 pm
Sunday: 10:00 am to 3:00 pm Sunday Brunch & Full Menu
Call anytime for Weddings, Family Reunions or a Weekend Stay at our
Beautiful 18-Room Rustic Boutique Inn**

## Bacon Wrapped Shrimp with Jalapeños & Pepper Jack Cheese Grits

6 large shrimp, peeled and deveined

6 bacon strips

Jalapeño, julienne slices

Cavender's Greek seasoning, to taste

Wrap a strip of bacon tightly around each shrimp with a slice of jalapeño. Season with Cavender's. Place on lined oven tray and bake at 375° for 15 minutes. Turn and cook 10 minutes more.

### Pepper Jack Cheese Grits:

3 cups water

1 tablespoon chicken base

½ cup diced red bell pepper (seeds removed)

6 (1-ounce) packets plain instant grits

1½ cups shredded Pepper Jack cheese

Boil water and chicken base; add bell pepper. Stir in grits and mix well. Add cheese and mix until melted. Serve topped with bacon wrapped shrimp.

**Chef Steve Mitchell**

## Smoke Tenderloin Stroganoff

1 (4-ounce) center-cut tenderloin

2 tablespoons butter

¾ cup sliced mushrooms

2 tablespoons chopped yellow onion

½ teaspoon chopped garlic

½ ounce red wine (1 tablespoon)

½ cup heavy cream

½ cup sour cream

½ teaspoon beef base or bouillon

½ teaspoon Worcestershire sauce

2 tablespoons marinara sauce

8 ounces fettuccini, cooked

½ teaspoon chopped fresh chives

Cut beef into 2-inch strips, and sear 5 minutes on hot grill; set aside. Heat butter in sauté pan over medium heat. Add mushrooms, onion and garlic; sweat until onions are transparent. Add meat to pan and cook 2 minutes. Deglaze with wine. Add cream; reduce by half. Add sour cream, beef base, Worcestershire and marinara; mix well. Cook 3 minutes. Heat fettuccini in a water bath for 1 minute. Drain and add to pan. Toss and garnish with chives.

**Chef Steve Mitchell**

# The Pecan Shed

**www.pecanshed.com**

**HENRIETTA LOCATION:**
808 US 287 South
Henrietta, TX 76365
940-538-0283

7 days a week: 6:00 am to 10:00 pm

In 1981, the Montz family opened the Pecan Shed. While it started off small, the Montz's currently have two retail locations, farm over 1,000 acres, growing more than 25,000 pecan trees, and ship pecans worldwide. The Pecan Shed in Henrietta is their latest endeavor. Customers can smell and taste all the fresh homemade goodies this store has to offer— everything from fudge, brittle, and pecan pies to candied pecans, pralines, and cinnamon rolls made right before your eyes. If you are traveling through Texas along Highway 287, the Pecan Shed will definitely be the best stop of your trip.

**WICHITA FALLS LOCATION:**
1401 Midwestern Parkway
Wichita Falls, TX 76302
940-322-0756

Monday – Saturday: 9:00 am to 5:00 pm

## Pecan Brownie Bites

1 (18-ounce) package chocolate fudge cake mix

¾ cup firmly packed brown sugar

¾ cup butter or margarine, melted

2 eggs

2 cups chopped Pecan Shed pecans

Spray a 9x13-inch baking pan. In a large mixing bowl, combine cake mix and brown sugar. Add butter and eggs; beat with electric mixer at medium speed for 3 to 4 minutes. Stir in nuts; mix completely. Spread batter evenly into pan (batter will be stiff). Bake at 350° for 35 to 40 minutes. Cool completely in pan and cut into bite-size pieces.

**Pecan Shed Recipe**

## Cheesecake Pecan Pie

1 (8-ounce) package cream cheese, softened

⅓ cup plus ¼ cup sugar, divided

2 teaspoons vanilla extract, divided

1 (9-inch) deep-dish pie crust

1 cup chopped Pecan Shed pecans

3 eggs, beaten

1 cup white Karo syrup

½ cup evaporated milk

Preheat oven to 375°. In a medium bowl, blend together cream cheese, ⅓ cup sugar and 1 teaspoon vanilla. When mixture is smooth, spread into bottom of pie shell. Sprinkle chopped Pecan Shed pecans on top of cream cheese layer. In another medium bowl, combine eggs, remaining ¼ cup sugar, corn syrup, evaporated milk and remaining 1 teaspoon vanilla extract. Whisk until mixture is smooth. Pour mixture over pecan layer. Bake 35 to 40 minutes, until set in center.

**Pecan Shed Recipe**

## Aunt Bebe's Pecan Pie

3 eggs, beaten

1 cup sugar

1 cup white Karo syrup

1 teaspoon vanilla

½ stick butter

1 cup Pecan Shed pecans

1 (8-inch) unbaked pie shell

Combine all ingredients, except pie shell. Pour into pie shell. Bake 10 minutes at 400°. Turn oven down to 350°. Bake until crust is brown and sides are firm but center jiggles, 35 to 45 minutes.

**Pecan Shed Recipe**

# The Red Onion Cafe

**1206 East Main Street**
**Honey Grove, TX 75446**
**903-378-3000**
**Find us on Facebook**

The Red Onion—what a name. Right? This is Debbie's first restaurant, and she struggled to find a name; this was the winner. The doors were opened May 2007 in a small town in the middle of nowhere. Since there were no nearby restaurants when it opened, the menu is large. The Red Onion serves home-style cooking using fresh meats and ingredients. You will enjoy the best homemade pies all made from scratch. The burgers are the best you can find, and a local favorite is the hand-battered, fresh beef cutlets for chicken-fried steaks. You will also find deli food, Mexican dishes, and even pizza. Check out the daily lunch specials, fish on Fridays, rib-eyes on Saturdays, and more. When you combine the great food with the wonderful staff, The Red Onion is worth the drive. There is "Something for Everyone."

**7 Days a Week: 7:00 am to 8:00 pm**

## Homemade Onion Rings

2 cups corn flour

4 tablespoons cayenne pepper

Yellow onions, sliced and separated into rings

1 (12-ounce) can evaporated milk

Mix corn flour and cayenne pepper together. Dip onions in evaporated milk then in corn flour, then re-dip in both. Fry in hot oil at 350° until golden brown.

**Restaurant Recipe**

## Chicken Pot Pie

2 pie crusts, unbaked

¼ cup oil

1 cup diced onion

3 potatoes, diced

3 (16-ounce) packages frozen mixed vegetables, thawed

6 chicken breasts, boiled and shredded in small pieces

3 (10.75-ounce) cans cream of chicken soup

Salt and pepper to taste

Lawry's Seasoned Salt

Line pan with one pie crust; bake at 400° until browned. Put oil in saucepan. Add onion and potatoes; sauté until lightly browned. Add thawed vegetables; sauté. Put in a large bowl; add chicken, soup, salt, pepper and seasoned salt. Mix well. Pour into baked pie crust; cover with second pie crust. Bake at 400° for 45 minutes to 1 hour or until golden brown.

**Restaurant Recipe**

## Meatloaf

2 pounds ground beef

2 (2-ounce) packages dry onion soup mix

2 cups chopped bell pepper

1 cup chopped onion

2 (8-ounce) cans tomato sauce, divided

3 eggs, beaten

Salt and pepper to taste

Mix all but 1 can tomato sauce together. Spread remaining 1 can tomato sauce on top; cook uncovered at 375° for 90 minutes.

**Restaurant Recipe**

# Mom's Café

**417 North Sealy Avenue**
**Justin, TX 76247**
**940-648-2581**
**www.momscafeinjustin.com**
**Find us on Facebook**

Welcome to Mom's Café, where friends and family meet for a taste of down-home cookin'. Enjoy a true, family-run café in a nonsmoking environment, and a dining experience enjoyed by customers and staff alike. Constant menu choices like chicken-fried steak, meatloaf, fish, burgers, and homemade pies abound. Each are special because the recipes are the same as since the café was built. This is just like sitting at Grandma's table where you get the feeling of "too full to move" as you enjoy that last bite of homemade pie. You'll be glad you visited.

**Monday – Friday: 8:00 am to 8:30 pm**
**Saturday: 7:00 am to 9:30 pm**

## Carrot Raisin Salad

2 cups shredded carrots

2 cups raisins

1 cup sugar

3 tablespoons mayonnaise

Mix all ingredients together. Serve.

**Family Favorite**

## English Pea Salad

1 (15-ounce) can English peas, drained

1 egg, boiled and diced

1 tomato, cubed

Salt and pepper to taste

¼ cup sugar

1 cup relish

3 tablespoons mayonnaise

Mix all ingredients together. Serve.

**Family Favorite**

## Chicken Spaghetti

5 pounds boneless skinless chicken breasts

1 teaspoon salt

1 teaspoon pepper

1 teaspoon garlic

1 teaspoon lemon pepper

1 (32-ounce) package spaghetti noodles

1 (4-ounce) can diced green chiles

2 cups sour cream

2 (23-ounce) cans cream of chicken soup

4 cups shredded cheese, divided

Boil chicken in water to cover with salt, pepper, garlic and lemon pepper until done; cut in cubes. Cook spaghetti per package directions; drain. Place in a large baking pan. In a large bowl, mix chicken, green chiles, sour cream, soup and 2 cups cheese; pour over spaghetti; stir. Top with remaining cheese. Bake at 350° for 40 to 45 minutes.

**Restaurant Recipe**

## Banana Pudding

1 (1.5-ounce) package sugar-free Jell-O vanilla instant pudding

2 cups skim milk (or 2% milk)

1 cup light Cool Whip

3 bananas

10 to 14 vanilla wafers

Prepare pudding as directed on package in a cool bowl; fold in Cool Whip. Layer bananas in the pudding and top with vanilla wafers. Refrigerate 30 minutes before serving.

**Restaurant Recipe**

# Good Times Cajun Cuisine

**1565 West Main Street**
**Lewisville, TX 75067**
**469-464-3033**
**www.goodtimescajun.com**

Good Times Cajun Cuisine truly lives up to its name. This is the best place outside of Louisiana for authentic Cajun cooking. They work hard to bring true Cajun flavor to their dishes like gumbo, red beans and rice, jambalaya, and other Cajun delights. They are noted as serving the best fried catfish anywhere, and don't forget the beignets. You would be hard-pressed to find a restaurant to beat Good Times, lovingly run by Brenda, who acknowledges the huge support and encouragement from her husband Allen and her three children, Benjamin and wife Lauren, Jonathon, and Lorianne. So drop by today and "Let the good times roll."

**Tuesday – Thursday: 11:00 am to 8:00 pm**
**Friday & Saturday: 11:00 am to 9:00 pm**

## Brenda's Bread Pudding

*Blue Ribbon Winner*

**6 eggs**

**3 cups sugar**

**1 quart heavy cream**

**1 cup brown sugar**

**1 tablespoon pure vanilla extract**

**⅛ cup cinnamon**

**1 cup raisins**

**4 loaves bread, 1-inch cubes**

**1 cup butter, melted and divided**

Preheat oven to 350°. By hand, mix eggs and sugar together. Add cream; mix well. Add brown sugar, vanilla, cinnamon and raisins. Slowly add bread; gently mix. Add ¾ cup butter. Use remaining ¼ cup butter to grease a 13½x18½-inch pan. Pour bread pudding into pan and bake 30 to 45 minutes, or until toothpick inserted in middle comes out clean.

### Bourbon Sauce:

**2 sticks butter**

**½ cup sugar**

**½ cup brown sugar**

**1 teaspoon cinnamon**

**1 teaspoon pure vanilla extract**

**¼ cup bourbon**

Melt butter in a saucepan over medium-low heat. Add both sugars, and mix well. Add cinnamon, vanilla and bourbon; cook 5 minutes. Cool, then drizzle over warm bread pudding.

**Restaurant Recipe**

## Aunt Helen's Almost Famous Brownies

*Aunt Helen baked these every summer when I visited her in Hueytown, Alabama. She doesn't bake anymore, but the sweet memories return each time I bake these brownies.*

**2 eggs**

**1 cup sugar**

**1 stick plus 2 tablespoons butter, melted**

**4 tablespoons cocoa**

**¾ cup all-purpose flour**

**½ teaspoon baking powder**

**⅛ teaspoon salt**

**1 teaspoon pure vanilla extract**

**1 cup chopped nuts**

Preheat oven 350°. Beat eggs and sugar. In a separate small bowl, combine melted butter and cocoa; stir into sugar mixture. Sift together flour, baking powder and salt. Add to chocolate mixture and mix well. Fold in vanilla and nuts. Bake in a buttered 9x9-inch dish for 30 minutes.

**Family Favorite**

# Natty Flat Smokehouse

**19280 US-281 South**
**Lipan, TX 76462**
**254-646-3844**
**www.txhcountry.com/smokehouse/**
**www.facebook.com/natty.smokehouse**

Natty Flat Smokehouse is located next door to Texas Hill Country Furniture and the world's largest rocking chair, registered with the "Guinness Book of World Records." There is a down-home country feel that provides visitors with delicious foods and a warm welcome. The restaurant offers barbeque meats, sandwiches, and plates. The General Store is stocked with Texas-made products and a variety of jams, sauces, and seasonings. Be sure to try one of the old-fashioned malts or milkshakes. You will leave feeling like a part of their family tradition.

**Monday – Thursday:**
**10:00 am to 7:30 pm**

**Friday & Saturday:**
**10:00 am to 8:00 pm**

**Sunday: 10:00 am to 6:00 pm**

## *Natty Flat Chili*

2 pounds ground sausage

5 pounds lean ground beef

1 large onion, chopped fine

6 to 7 pounds peeled, deseeded and crushed tomatoes (or 1 [3-quart] can crushed tomatoes)

4 ounces chili powder

2 tablespoons seasoned salt

2 tablespoons garlic powder

2 tablespoons cumin

1 tablespoon cayenne

1 tablespoon black pepper

In a large saucepan, brown sausage, ground beef and onion over high heat, stirring frequently, until brown, about 20 minutes. Add remaining ingredients and mix well. Bring to a boil then reduce to medium-low heat and simmer 30 minutes, stirring occasionally.

**Restaurant Recipe**

## *Baked Potato Salad*

2 pounds russet potatoes
(about 6 medium potatoes)

½ cup mayonnaise

¾ cup sour cream

½ cup butter, softened

2 tablespoons salt

2 tablespoons black pepper

1 cup bacon crumbles, divided

1 cup shredded Cheddar cheese, divided

Wrap potatoes in foil and bake 1 to 1½ hours at 350°. Cool. Peel baked potatoes and mash. In a large bowl, make dressing by combining mayo, sour cream, butter, salt and black pepper. Stir half the bacon and half the cheese into potatoes. Pour dressing over top and stir to combine. Garnish Baked Potato Salad with remaining bacon and cheese immediately before serving.

**Restaurant Recipe**

# River Smith's
# Chicken & Catfish

**406 Avenue Q • Lubbock, TX 79401**
**806-765-8164 • www.riversmiths.com**

River Smith's Chicken & Catfish is a family-owned restaurant specializing in fried catfish, chicken, and more since 1976. If you are looking for a healthier option, the menu delivers with grilled burgers plus charbroiled and blackened items. River Smith's has been honored with the "Top Performer Award" and two "Best of Lubbock" awards. You will feel at home in their friendly, nonsmoking atmosphere with TVs and an 1,800-gallon aquarium.

Sunday – Tuesday: 11:00 am to 9:00 pm
Wednesday – Saturday: 11:00 am to 10:00 pm

## Green Pea Salad

2 (101-ounce) cans green peas

1 (15-ounce) can diced red peppers

3 cups diced red onions, ¼ inch dice

8 cups shredded Cheddar cheese

8 cups Miracle Whip

Drain peas, rinse, drain again and set aside. Drain peppers. Mix all ingredients, except peas, together; fold in peas. Store in airtight container. Store and serve at 41° or less.

**Restaurant Recipe**

## Vinegar Cucumber Salad

5½ cups sugar

1½ quarts vinegar

1 tablespoon black pepper

1 red onion, thinly sliced

3 to 4 cucumbers, thinly sliced

Combine sugar, vinegar and pepper to dissolve sugar; set aside. Place onion and cucumbers in a large bowl or plastic container. Cover with marinade. Set aside to marinate 2 to 2½ hours before serving.

**Restaurant Recipe**

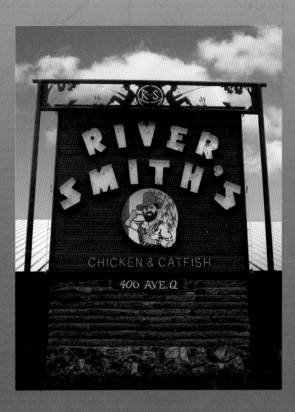

## Tartar Sauce

1 gallon Miracle Whip

4 cups dill relish

4 cups sweet relish

¾ cup minced yellow onions

Drain relish well. Mix all ingredients with VCM (or hand blender) until well mixed. Cover in airtight container; store at 41°.

**Restaurant Recipe**

# Tommy's Famous Burgers

**117 University Avenue**
**Lubbock, TX 79415**
**806-763-5424**
**www.tommysfamousburgers.com**

Tommy's Famous Burgers is an authentic, old-fashioned burger joint that has been family owned for 40 years. The meat is delivered fresh daily, never frozen. The veggies are cut fresh every morning. The menu includes not only burgers, but Frito pies, chili cheese dogs, chicken-fried steak, and a number of other choices. For dessert, choose from the wide variety of ice cream desserts. The Texas Tech football stadium is just three blocks away. Come see them for the best burger in town, and say hi to Tony, Terry, and Carson.

**7 days a week: 10:00 am to 11:00 pm**

## Baklava
### (Traditional Greek Pastry)

*Syrup:*

**3 cups sugar**

**1½ cups water**

**½ lemon, juiced**

**1 cup honey**

In a saucepan, boil sugar, water and lemon juice 10 minutes. Reduce heat and slowly add honey; simmer 5 minutes. Set aside to cool.

**1 pound ground pecans**

**½ cup sugar**

**2 teaspoons cinnamon**

**4 sticks butter, melted and clarified**

**1 pound filo dough**

**Whole cloves (optional)**

Combine pecans, sugar and cinnamon; set aside. Line bottom of buttered 9x13-inch baking pan with 10 to 12 filo sheets, brushing each with butter. Sprinkle with ¼ of nut mixture. Repeat to make 4 layers. Cover with remaining buttered filo. Refrigerate 25 minutes. Cut into small diamond shapes. Brush with butter and insert 1 clove in center of each piece. Bake at 325° for 1 to 1½ hours until slightly browned. Slowly pour enough cooled syrup over hot baklava until completely absorbed.

**Family Favorite**

## Souvlaki
### (Grilled Pork Kabobs)

**2 pounds pork tenderloin, 1 inch cubed**

**½ cup lemon juice**

**¼ cup olive oil**

**2 tablespoons oregano**

**2 tablespoons chopped garlic**

**Wooden skewers**

In a bowl, toss together pork, lemon juice, olive oil, oregano and garlic. Marinate 4 hours or overnight. Place 6 cubes meat on each skewer. Cook on hot grill until done. Serve with grilled pita bread, sliced red onion, and Roma tomatoes and top with Tzatziki sauce.

**Family Favorite**

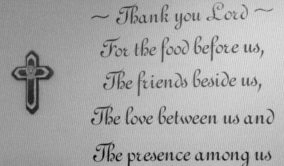

~ Thank you Lord ~
For the food before us,
The friends beside us,
The love between us and
The presence among us

# Gilda's Grill

**901 East Highway 90 West**
**Marathon, TX 79842**
**432-386-4238**

After a fire destroyed the business in 2013, Gilda's went back to the heart of the matter. The family were pioneers in far west Texas, and the values that allowed them to carve a home out of the desert and thrive are the same values lived by in the restaurant today—hospitality to strangers and neighbors, honest value, and lots of good, fresh, soul-satisfying cooking. Gilda's Grill has a brand-new home, but inside it's still the same—generations working together to bring the best to the community, from their family to yours.

**Monday – Saturday: 6:45 am to 6:30 pm**

## Gilda's Gorditas

**2½ cups masa harina**

**1 teaspoon salt**

**1½ cups oil plus more for prep service**

**1½ cups warm water**

In a large bowl, stir together harina, salt, oil and water. If dough seems dry, add a little more warm water. Form dough into balls that will fit into the palm of your hand. Line work surface with wax paper, sprinkled with oil so dough won't stick. Flatten balls on oiled surface to ¼-inch thickness. Heat griddle to medium heat. Griddle gorditas on each side until cooked through. Heat oil in large skillet over medium-high heat. Fry gorditas on both sides until golden. Drain; dry on paper towels. Fill with your favorite food—seasoned beef or chicken, beans, or vegetables.

**Restaurant Recipe**

## Aguilar Enchiladas

**5 red chile pods, stems and seeds removed**

**½ teaspoon salt**

**½ teaspoon garlic powder**

**½ teaspoon onion powder**

**2 tablespoons flour**

**3 tablespoons oil, divided**

**10 corn tortillas**

**3 cups shredded cheese**

**1 cup chopped onions**

In a small amount of water, boil chile pods until soft. Blend with water, salt, garlic powder and onion powder until smooth. Set aside. Add flour and 2 tablespoons oil in a saucepan; whisk until well-mixed. Add chile mixture; whisk until smooth. If sauce is too thick, add a little water. Heat remaining tablespoon oil in skillet; fry corn tortillas lightly, keeping them soft. Dip tortillas in sauce; put flat on plate, adding cheese and onions (or roll with cheese inside, and top with onions).

**Restaurant Recipe**

# Red River Steakhouse

**101 West Highway 66**
**McLean, TX 78057**
**806-779-8940**
**www.redriversteakhouse.com**

Y'all have just found one of the best kept secrets in Texas—Red River Steakhouse® in McLean, Texas, a place that embodies the spirit of the Wild West, the power of great hunters and the classic feel of Route 66. One of the most talked about steakhouses in Texas, the Red River Steakhouse® is a place you will always remember and return to every time you are in the area. The food quality and quantity is the best anywhere on Route 66. Try one of the world-famous hand-cut steaks, cut from the best choice Black Angus available, or enjoy the secret catfish recipe; your taste buds will be delighted. If you are in the mood for a hand-battered chicken-fried steak, Red River's is made like no other, cooked on the flat top, never deep-fried, for a tender mouthwatering steak you can really savor.

**Tuesday – Saturday: 11:00 am to 9:00 pm**

## Red River Chicken

**4 chicken breasts, butterflied**

**1 cup Italian dressing**

**1 jumbo yellow onion, sliced**

**1 tablespoon olive oil**

**4 Anaheim green chiles, peeled, roasted*, deseeded and diced**

**4 slices Jack cheese**

Preheat oven to 350°. Soak chicken in Italian dressing at least 4 hours in a 9x13-inch baking dish. Bake 45 minutes to 1 hour or until chicken reaches 160° internally. Sauté onions in olive oil in a skillet until golden brown. Place chiles, cheese and onions on top of the chicken and bake an additional 10 minutes to melt cheese before serving. Serves 4.

*To roast chiles, bake in oven at 450° until skin bubbles and turns dark. The skin will lift slightly off of the chile when cooled.

**Restaurant Recipe**

## Plum Cobbler

**½ cup unsalted butter**

**1 cup all-purpose flour**

**2 cups sugar, divided**

**1 cup brown sugar**

**1 tablespoon baking powder**

**Pinch salt**

**1 cup milk**

**4 cups fresh plum halves, pitted**

**Ground cinnamon to taste (optional)**

Melt butter in 9x13-inch baking dish. Combine flour, 1 cup sugar, brown sugar, baking powder and salt; add milk, stirring just until moistened. Pour batter over butter (do not stir). Bring remaining 1 cup sugar and plum halves to a boil over high heat, stirring constantly; pour over batter (do not stir). Sprinkle with cinnamon, if desired. Bake at 375° for 40 to 45 minutes or until golden brown. Serve warm or cool. Serves 4.

**Restaurant Recipe**

# Laura's Cheesecake & Bakery

**109 North Madison**
**Mount Pleasant, TX 75455**
**903-577-8177**
**www.laurascheesecakes.com**

Laura's Cheesecake & Bakery, established in 1987, is located in beautiful downtown Mount Pleasant. They have been on the west side of the town square serving lunch and shipping cheesecakes for more than 20 years. Laura's specializes in homemade soups, sandwiches, and salads, and each day features a lunch special. Visit the bakery where you will be able to enjoy a sinfully delicious slice of cheesecake, and an assortment of fresh baked cookies, breads, and gourmet foods.

**Monday – Friday: 10:00 am to 4:00 pm (Lunch: 11:00 am to 2:00 pm)**

## Sopapilla Cheesecake

2 (8-ounce) cans crescent rolls

2 (8-ounce) packages cream cheese, softened

1½ cups sugar

1 teaspoon vanilla

1 tablespoon cinnamon

3 tablespoons sugar

1 stick butter, melted

Press 1 can crescent rolls in 9x13-inch pan. Mix cream cheese, sugar and vanilla; spread on top of rolls. Lay second can of crescent rolls on top of cream cheese mixture. Combine cinnamon and sugar; sprinkle on top. Pour melted butter over top. Bake at 350° for 25 to 30 minutes. Remove from oven.

### Glaze:

1 cup powdered sugar

1 tablespoon milk

Vanilla, to taste

Mix and pour over warm cheesecake.

**Restaurant Recipe**

## Pasta Salad

1 (16-ounce) package tri-colored pasta

4 teaspoons seasoned salt

6 tablespoons lemon juice

1 cup canola or vegetable oil

1½ cups chopped celery

1 cup chopped bell pepper

1 medium white onion, chopped

2 small pimentos, chopped

2 (4-ounce) cans chopped ripe olives

1 cup mayonnaise

Cook pasta according to instructions on package. Add all remaining ingredients. Refrigerate overnight. Serve cold.

**Restaurant Recipe**

## Buttermilk Pound Cake

3 cups all-purpose flour

¼ teaspoon baking soda

1 cup butter, softened

3 cups sugar

4 eggs

1 cup buttermilk

1½ teaspoons vanilla

Mix flour and baking soda. In separate bowl, cream butter and sugar together. Add eggs one at a time; continuously beating, alternate adding flour mixture and buttermilk until well combined. Add vanilla; mix well. Bake at 350° for 1 hour.

**Restaurant Recipe**

# The Barn Café

**3320 Highway 82 East
Paris, TX 75461
903-739-2571**

The Barn Café, located in the Paris Livestock Auction Barn, is operated by sisters, Zane and Jennifer. They take great pride in the food they serve, from the hand-battered chicken-fried steak to the made-from-scratch pies and cakes. The sisters say, "Our favorite part of the business is hearing the phrase: 'I heard that I can get some good homemade food here.' A big 'Thank You' goes out to all who have supported us this first year of business. It has been great."

**Wednesday: 10:00 am to 4:00 pm
Thursday – Saturday: 4:00 pm to 9:00 pm**

## Squash Casserole

**10 pounds yellow squash,
sliced in rounds**

**2 large onions, chopped**

**½ cup real butter**

**Salt and pepper to taste**

**20 to 28 ounces buttered crackers,
crushed (divided)**

**2 to 3 pounds Velveeta cheese, cubed**

Place squash, onions, butter, salt and pepper in a large stockpot with water to cover; boil till tender. Transfer cooked squash and onions with some of the broth to a large baking pan that has been sprayed with cooking oil. Reserve 2 cups cracker crumbs for topping. Add Velveeta and remaining crackers to squash and stir lightly. Top with reserved cracker crumbs. Bake at 350° till bubbling and top is brown.

**Restaurant Recipe**

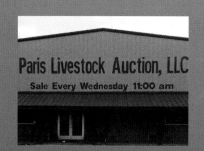

## Pinto Bean Pie

**¾ cup mashed cooked pinto beans**

**1½ cups sugar**

**½ cup real butter, melted**

**1 teaspoon vanilla**

**¾ cup chopped pecans**

**2 eggs, beaten**

**1 (9-inch) pie shell, unbaked**

Mix all together, except pie crust, by hand; do not beat. Pour into pie shell. Bake at 350° for 1 hour or until firm.

**Restaurant Recipe**

## Nanna's Chocolate Pie

**1½ cups sugar**

**3 heaping tablespoons flour**

**4 heaping tablespoons cocoa**

**2 cups milk**

**3 egg yolks, beaten**

**1½ teaspoons vanilla**

**1 (9-inch) pie shell, baked**

Mix dry ingredients together. Add milk, egg yolks, and vanilla; beat well with a whisk. Cook over medium heat on stovetop, stirring constantly, till thickened. Pour in baked shell. Cool then top with meringue or Cool Whip, if desired.

**Family Favorite**

# Burgerland

**1301 North Main • Paris, TX 75460**
**903-739-9443 • www.burgerlandparis.com**
**Find us on Facebook**

Since 1982, Burgerland has served their area in a small building with 20 bar stools around an L-shaped bar. Voted "Best Burger and Fries" by the *Paris News* readers' choice poll, they continually strive to be the best with great customer service and an atmosphere that people love. They also have a catering trailer used for events in town and surrounding areas. They use a fresh meat patty along with all fresh veggies and fresh-cut fries. "Once you have had the Best, you will not want the rest."

**Monday – Friday: 10:30 am to 8:00 pm**
**Saturday: 10:30 am to 4:00 pm**

## French Fries

**Freshly cut potatoes**

**House seasoning or seasoned salt**

**Shredded Cheddar cheese**

**Bacon, cooked and chopped**

Before frying, sprinkle potatoes with House seasoning. After fries are cooked, pile them on a container; add more house seasoning (we have not found anything this seasoning is not good on). Live on the edge by topping with cheese; melt it then pile on bacon. Watch them disappear.

**Restaurant Recipe**

## Old-Fashioned Burger

**1 fresh-ground beef patty**

**House seasoning**

**1 bun**

**Butter**

**Mustard**

**Mayonnaise**

**Pickles**

**Onion slice**

**Lettuce**

**Tomato slice**

**Cheese slice**

**Jalapeño, grilled**

**Bacon, cooked**

Fry patty, seasoned with house seasoning, on grill. Spread butter on bun; toast on the grill. Add mustard and mayonnaise to bottom bun. Layer on pickles, onion, lettuce and tomato. Add patty and cheese. Add grilled jalapeño and bacon for extra flare. Finish with top bun. Enjoy, but grab the napkins—you are going to need them.

**Restaurant Recipe**

# Old Mill BBQ and Burritos

**1318 South Eddy Street
Pecos, TX 79772
432-447-6106
www.oldmillbbqandburritos.com**

Old Mill BBQ and Burritos in Pecos was opened in 1947 by the current owner's grandfather, Amador Gochicoa, who started the restaurant with his goal of offering delicious American, Mexican, BBQ, and Italian foods. His son-in-law, Sebero Sr., took over the business in the 70s. After he retired, his son, Sebero Jaquez, Jr., took over the business in 1992 and then brought his son, Sebero Jaquez, III, into the business after graduating from culinary school. Sebero Jaquez, Jr., operates the family-owned business with his son Sebero Jaquez, combining culinary expertise and business acumen to make Old Mill BBQ & Burritos one of the most preferred restaurants in the area. Old Mill chefs prepare the food with passion for an amazing feast you'll remember for a long time. Catering is available for weddings or other special events; Old Mill will serve dishes your guests will absolutely love.

**Monday – Friday: 6:30 am to 8:00 pm
Saturday: 7:00 am to 2:00 pm**

## Asado

### Red New Mexico Chile Sauce:

**15 to 20 red New Mexico chile pods**

**2 cups water**

**Salt and garlic powder to taste**

Combine chile pods and water in a stockpot; bring to a boil and cook about 30 minutes or until pods become soft. Drain liquid and place chile pods in blender; blend about 15 minutes until mixture comes to a sauce consistency. Add salt and garlic powder to taste. Set aside.

### Asado:

**10 pounds pork, with fat trimmed, diced**

**Salt to taste**

**Garlic powder to taste**

**1 tablespoon dry oregano**

**2 cups all-purpose flour**

**Red New Mexico Chile Sauce**

Place diced pork, salt, garlic powder and oregano in a Dutch oven; add water to cover and cook 45 minutes or until tender. Add flour and cook 5 minutes. Add Red New Mexico Chili Sauce. Bring to a boil to thicken, then reduce heat to simmer and cook 30 minutes. Serves 10 to 20 people.

**Restaurant Recipe**

## Old Mill Brisket

**4 ounces garlic powder**

**2 ounces onion powder**

**4 ounces kosher salt**

**4 ounces black pepper**

**4 ounces paprika powder**

**1 brisket**

Mix all dry ingredients. Rub mixture all over brisket. Put brisket in mesquite smoker and cook 11 to 12 hours at 250°. Remove and rest 30 minutes. Slice and serve. Serves 10 to 15 people.

**Restaurant Recipe**

## Chili Verde con Carne

**10 pounds diced beef stew meat**

**2 to 3 onions, diced**

**Garlic to taste**

**Dry oregano to taste**

**Salt to taste**

**15 to 20 roasted jalapeños, small diced**

**2 cups water**

**2 cups all-purpose flour**

Cook beef, onions, garlic and oregano in a skillet for 45 minutes to 1 hour or until meat is tender. Season to taste with salt. Add jalapeños and cook 5 to 10 minutes longer. Add water and flour; bring to a boil to thicken. Simmer 30 to 45 minutes. Serves 10 to 20 people.

**Restaurant Recipe**

# Baby Butt's BBQ

**1702 South Main**
**Perryton, TX 79070**
**806-648-1696**

Baby Butt's is at the "Top of Texas"—on the map and on the charts. You won't find BBQ like this anywhere else. They cook the meats slow to perfection, just the way you like it. Add the homemade BBQ sauce for that extra kick, and don't forget to get a side of the famous cheesy rig taters. All sides are homemade and taste like it just came from your momma's kitchen. Friday nights, enjoy a fantastic catfish and chicken buffet with all the fixin's, including their popular homemade mac and cheese. Or try the melt in your mouth smoked turkey...it's a

 town favorite. For light eaters, they offer a great all-you-can-eat salad bar. So come on, and they'll "See ya at the TOP."

**Monday – Friday:**
**11:00 am to 8:00 pm**

## *Meatloaf*

**2 pounds ground beef**
**1 onion, chopped**
**1 bell pepper, chopped**
**2 eggs, slightly beaten**
**1 (12-ounce) can diced tomatoes or Rotel tomatoes**
**1 (8-ounce) can tomato sauce**
**1 cup cracker crumbs**
**Salt, pepper and garlic to taste**
**1 (10.75-ounce) can tomato soup for topping**

Preheat oven to 350°. Mix all ingredients together, except soup. Form a loaf and place in loaf pan. Bake 45 minutes. Pour grease from pan. Pour tomato soup over loaf and bake another 30 minutes; this will make a gravy-like sauce. Serve with your favorite side.

**Family Favorite**

## Corn Casserole

1 stick margarine

1 onion, chopped

2 (4-ounce) cans green chiles

2 (15-ounce) cans whole-kernel corn, drained

2 (15-ounce) cans cream-style corn

2 eggs, lightly beaten

1 sleeve saltine crackers, crushed

1 pound shredded Cheddar cheese

Salt and pepper to taste

Melt margarine in a skillet over medium heat; sauté onion and green chiles. In a mixing bowl, add all corn (drain water off whole-kernel corn), eggs, crackers and cheese. Mix in sautéed onion and chiles; season to taste with salt and pepper. Put in 9x13-inch pan and bake at 350° for 1 hour.

**Family Favorite**

## Chicken Chili

1 tablespoon vegetable oil

1 onion, chopped

3 cloves garlic, crushed

1 (4-ounce) can diced jalapeño peppers

1 (4-ounce) can chopped green chiles

2 teaspoons ground cumin

1 teaspoon dried oregano (Mexican oregano works best)

1 teaspoon ground cayenne pepper

2 (14.5-ounce) cans chicken broth

3 cups chopped or shredded cooked chicken breast

3 (15-ounce) cans Great Northern white beans

1 cup shredded Monterey or Pepper Jack cheese

Heat oil in a large saucepan over medium-low heat. Add onion; slowly cook and stir until tender. Mix in garlic, jalapeño, green chiles, cumin, oregano and cayenne. Continue to cook and stir mixture until tender. Mix in broth, chicken and white beans. Simmer 15 minutes, stirring occasionally. Remove from heat. Slowly stir in cheese until melted. Best served with tortilla chips or crackers.

**Family Favorite**

## Bayou Catfish

**7 ounce domestic catfish fillet**
**Blackening seasoning to taste**
**Flour for coating**
**Salt and pepper to taste**

Coat 1 side of catfish with blackening seasoning. Lightly bread fillet with seasoned flour. Fry in hot oil to golden brown. Serve covered with gravy.

### Jalapeño Cream Gravy:

**2 tablespoons drippings**
**from fried chicken**
**2 tablespoons flour**
**1 jalapeño pepper, seeded and diced**
**1⅔ cups milk**
**Salt and pepper to taste**

Heat drippings in a skillet. Add flour and jalapeño; mix well. Slowly add milk while stirring constantly. Season with salt and pepper. Cook until thickened.

**Restaurant Recipe**

# Bayou Jack's Cajun Grill

**200 North Oak Street**
**Roanoke, TX 76262**
**817-490-7800**
**www.bayoujackscajungrill.com**

Bayou Jack's Cajun Grill in Roanoke is reminiscent of a New Orleans experience with a casual, relaxed, and warm atmosphere featuring the finest seafood and Cajun cuisine. The menu showcases traditional Cajun classics with a few twists to other fine dishes. Every meal should begin with a cup of their famous Gumbo; hot, dark roux with shrimp, chicken, andouille sausage, okra, and a pinch of this and that will have you begging for more. Then it's time for the signature appetizer—DIRTY BALLS. You can't go wrong with any of the classics, such as crawfish étouffée, shrimp grits, or Louisiana pot roast po'boy, which will surely make you reach over and slap your momma.

**Sunday – Thursday: 11:00 am to 10:00 pm**
**Friday & Saturday: 11:00 am to 11:00 pm**

## Crawfish Ètouffée

1 cup each: chopped yellow onion, chopped green bell pepper, chopped celery

1 tablespoon chopped garlic

4 tablespoons butter

½ tablespoon blackening seasoning

½ tablespoon white pepper

1½ teaspoons cayenne pepper

1 tablespoon black pepper

1 tablespoon oregano

2 teaspoons thyme

¼ cup white wine

2 tablespoons tomato paste

2 tablespoons Worcestershire sauce

3 tablespoons shrimp base

½ cup all-purpose flour

4 tablespoons oil

4 pounds frozen crawfish tail meat

In sauté pan, cook onion, bell pepper, celery and garlic in butter until veggies are soft. Transfer to large stockpot. Add seasonings, wine, tomato paste, Worcestershire, shrimp base and ½ gallon water; mix well. Bring to a boil over high heat; reduce to a simmer. In a small stockpot, brown flour in oil over medium heat just until light brown; do not burn. Add 1 quart cold water and mix well. Increase to medium-high heat and cook until mixture thickens; do not burn. Add to vegetable mixture; mix well. Add crawfish tails and cook until crawfish tails are cooked through.

**Restaurant Recipe**

## Shrimp & Crawfish Ceviche

½ quart water

¾ quart ketchup

¼ cup freshly squeezed lime juice

1 tablespoon Worcestershire sauce

¼ cup red Tabasco sauce

¼ cup Cajun Chef hot sauce

1 quart diced yellow onions

1 quart fresh Roma tomatoes, diced

1 ounce minced fresh jalapeños

1 cup chopped fresh cilantro

3 avocados, cubed

3 cups chopped boiled shrimp

3 cups chopped boiled crawfish tails (frozen works fine)

Mix all ingredients together.

**Restaurant Recipe**

# Jack & Grill

## Grilled Wings and Things

**301 South Oak Street, Suite 200**
**Roanoke, TX 76262**
**682-831-1177 • www.jackgrill.com**

Welcome to Jack & Grill, your neighborhood sports hangout with a lineup you can't refuse! They pride themselves in creating each dish with the flavors other sports bars seem to forget. For starters, everyone should try the Marinated Smoked Grilled Wings with sauces ranging from Sissy to Jack You Up. If wings ain't your thing, then you can rock with the Pulled Pork Nachos or the newest addition to the menu, TOTS. And everyone loves our TOTS. House-made jalapeño/Cheddar mashed potatoes, lightly breaded and fried. And yes, they have all your favorite bar foods, but this IS NOT BAR FOOD. You'll leave wanting more, and did I forget to mention the 53 Craft beers on TAP? Such as Dogfish Heads, Odell's, Deep Elams, Grapevines, Shannon's, and sooo much more that you'll want to TAP Jack & Grill every day.

**Sunday – Thursday: 11:00 am to 10:00 pm**
**Friday & Saturday: 11:00 am to 11:00 pm**

## Tots

**Prepared mashed potatoes**
**(your favorite recipe)**

**Soda water**

**Seasoned flour**

**Oil for frying**

Line a cooking sheet with wax paper and spread mashed potatoes evenly over pan; freeze. When frozen, cut into small squares. Place in a wash bath of soda water and coat with seasoned flour. Repeat breading process then fry to golden brown in hot oil.

**Restaurant Recipe**

## Pulled Pork Sliders

**5 pound pork roast**

**Dry rub**

**Prepared mustard**

**Liquid smoke**

**Sweet slider bun**

**Prepared coleslaw**

**Barbecue sauce**

Cover roast with dry rub, mustard and liquid smoke. Place in oven-safe container and cover bottom with water. Cover and place in oven at 350° for 8 hours. After cooling to the touch, pull meat apart. Place 2 ounces meat on a sweet slider bun and top with coleslaw and barbecue sauce.

**Restaurant Recipe**

## Marinated Smoked Grilled Wings

**Chicken wings**

**Red hot sauce**

Marinate wings in red hot sauce for 24 hours. Place in smoker for 1 hour at 200°. Immediately after smoking, place on 450° grill until charred.

**Restaurant Recipe**

## Black and Bleu Burger

**1 (8-ounce) ground beef patty**

**Blackened seasoning**

**Sweet hamburger buns**

**Bleu cheese crumbles**

**Wing sauce**

**Lettuce, tomato slice, onion slice, pickles**

Season patty with blackened seasoning on both sides. Cook on grill over a fire or griddle until cooked to your desired heat. Place on bun and top with bleu cheese crumbles and your favorite wing sauce. Add lettuce, tomato, onion and pickles. Serve immediately.

**Restaurant Recipe**

# Cornuda's Café

**82701 US 180-62**
**Salt Flat, TX 79847**
**915-964-2508**

Cornuda Café has four redeeming features. First, May Carson, who owns the place (and the six-unit motel and RV park outback), just happens to be the mayor, population 6. Second, a gaggle of more than 400 baseball caps hang from the rafters. Third, enjoy the cozy, neighborly ambience. Fourth, the grilled burgers, crowned with fleshy green chile pods and melted Cheddar cheese, make the chains shudder in fright. Don't forget to drop in the gift shop full of handcrafts, notecards and interesting object d'art. Come by in May for the chili cook off to benefit the "Reach for a Star" foundation and enter the Goose Poop contest. (Don't ask!)

**Wednesday – Friday: 8:00 am to 7:00 pm**
**Saturday: 8:00 am to 6:00 pm**
**Sunday: 10:00 am to 6:00 pm**

## Overnight Stuffed Texas Toast

**20 pieces Texas toast**

**1 (8-ounce) package cream cheese, softened**

**3 cups egg substitute**

**2 cups milk**

**⅓ cup plus 1¾ cups sugar-free maple syrup, divided**

**1 teaspoon vanilla extract**

**¼ teaspoon ground cinnamon**

**2½ cups sliced fresh strawberries**

Arrange 10 slices bread in a 9x13-inch baking dish coated with nonstick cooking spray. Spread each slice with cream cheese. Top with remaining bread. In a large bowl, combine egg substitute, milk, ⅓ cup syrup, vanilla and cinnamon. Pour over bread. Cover and refrigerate overnight. Remove from refrigerator 30 minutes before baking. Bake uncovered at 350° for 45 to 50 minutes or until top is lightly browned and thermometer reads 160°. Serve with sliced strawberries and remaining syrup.

**Restaurant Recipe**

## My Texas Sheet Cake

**2 cups sugar**

**2 cups all-purpose flour**

**1 teaspoon cinnamon**

**1 teaspoon baking soda**

**1 stick butter**

**½ cup Crisco shortening**

**4 tablespoons cocoa**

**1 cup water**

**½ cup buttermilk**

**1 teaspoon vanilla**

**2 eggs, lightly beaten**

Grease and flour a 10x16-inch pan. In large bowl, sift together sugar, flour, cinnamon and baking soda. In saucepan, bring butter, shortening, cocoa and water to a boil. Pour over sugar-flour mixture; beat well. Add buttermilk, vanilla and eggs; beat well. Pour into pan. Bake 20 to 25 minutes at 350°. Five minutes before cake is done, start frosting.

### *Frosting:*

**6 tablespoons milk**

**3 tablespoons cocoa**

**1 stick butter**

**½ cup chopped nuts**

**1 (16-ounce) box powdered sugar**

**½ cup grated coconut**

In saucepan, bring butter, milk and cocoa to a boil. Remove from heat and add nuts, powdered sugar and coconut; beat to frosting consistency. Cool cake 5 minutes (only) before frosting. Makes 40 bars.

**Restaurant Recipe**

# Silo House Restaurant

**2503 Martin Luther King Boulevard
San Angelo, TX 76903
325-658-3333
www.silohouse.net
Find us on Facebook**

SILO HOUSE RESTAURANT, the best hidden treasure in Texas, is located in an old abandoned chicken farm built in and around the original grain silos. You never know what delights the chef may have on any given day from a five-course meal—Thursday through Saturday evenings—to the bistro-style lunches—Tuesday through Friday—both offer a hands-on approach providing the best food possible. All ingredients are from local suppliers, and some herbs and vegetables are actually grown next to the restaurant in their own garden. Don't forget Helen's world-famous bread pudding. There is always a surprise to entice even the pickiest of dessert connoisseurs.

Tuesday – Friday: 11:00 am to 2:00 pm
Thursday – Saturday: 6:00 pm to 10:00 pm

## Sour Cream Chicken Enchiladas

2 cups chicken broth

2 cups milk

Lawry's Seasoned Salt

White pepper

Granulated garlic

¾ cup flour

½ cup melted margarine

1 cup sour cream

12 corn tortillas

3 cups shredded chicken

1 cup grated Monterey Jack cheese, divided

12 jalapeño peppers, sliced

¼ cup chopped green onions

In saucepan, heat chicken broth and milk; add seasoned salt, white pepper and garlic to taste. In another saucepan, melt margarine and stir in flour. When milk mixture is almost boiling, whisk in flour mixture to thicken sauce. When sauce thickens, turn off heat; stir in sour cream. Dip each tortilla in sauce; divide chicken evenly on tortillas. Roll tortillas; place in well-greased baking dish. Spoon one-half of sauce over top; sprinkle with ½ cup grated Jack cheese and jalapeños. Cover dish with aluminum foil. Bake at 350° for 30 minutes. Serve with additional sauce and cheese. Garnish with chopped green onions.

**Restaurant Recipe**

## Butternut Squash Bisque

1 tablespoon canola oil

1 tablespoon unsalted butter

½ cup diced onion

¾ cup diced carrots

4 cups peeled and cubed butternut squash

3 cups vegetable stock

Salt and ground black pepper to taste

Ground nutmeg to taste

1½ cups heavy cream

In large pot over medium heat, add oil; melt butter. Add onion; cook until tender. Add carrots and squash. Pour in stock; season with salt, pepper and nutmeg. Bring to a boil. Reduce heat; simmer until vegetables are tender. In a blender, purée mixture until smooth. Return to pot; stir in cream. Heat through; do not boil. Serve warm with a dash of nutmeg. To garnish, swirl with sour cream and top with crisp bacon.

**Restaurant Recipe**

# Zentner's Daughter Steak House

**1901 Knickerbocker Road**
**San Angelo, TX 76904**
**325-949-2821**
**www.zentnersdaughter.com**

Betty Zentner was working in a department store in 1974 when she was presented with the opportunity to open Zentner's Daughter, her San Angelo restaurant. By then, the Zentner name was well known in west Texas because Betty's father, John Zentner (1899–1994), opened a number of popular steakhouses throughout the region. True to the Zentner family tradition, the restaurant primarily focuses on its steaks. The restaurant's interior pays tribute to the

Zentner legacy, with rooms named after Betty's relatives, and walls adorned with paintings and pictures of family. Come in and eat some of the best steaks to ever pass through your lips.

**Every Day: 11:00 am to 2:00 pm**
**Sunday – Thursday: 5:00 pm to 9:00 pm**
**Friday & Saturday: 5:00 pm to 11:00 pm**

## Country-Fried Steak

**2 cups all-purpose flour**
**2 teaspoons salt**
**¼ teaspoon black pepper**
**2 cups milk**
**4 (4-ounce) cube steaks**
**Vegetable oil for frying**

Sift flour, salt and pepper together in large shallow bowl. Pour milk into another bowl. Trim steaks of any fat, then flatten out with your hand. Dredge each steak first in milk, then in flour mixture. Repeat to coat each steak twice. Place on wax paper and freeze several hours until solid. Prepare gravy 10 minutes before frying steaks.

### Gravy:

**1½ tablespoons ground beef**
**¼ cup all-purpose flour**
**2 cups chicken stock**
**2 cups whole milk**
**¼ teaspoon black pepper**
**¼ teaspoon salt**

In medium saucepan, brown beef over medium heat, crumbling as it cooks. Stir in flour. Add remaining ingredients and boil 1 minute, stirring often. Simmer 10 to 15 minutes until thick. Keep warm.

In a deep frying pan, add oil to cover steaks; heat to 350°. Fry steaks one at a time for 8 to 10 minutes or until golden brown. Drain on paper towels. Serve steaks with gravy poured over top.

**Restaurant Recipe**

## "Fried" Ice Cream

**2 (6-inch) flour tortillas**
**½ cup vegetable oil**
**½ teaspoon ground cinnamon**
**2 tablespoons sugar**
**¼ cup cornflake crumbs**
**2 large scoops vanilla ice cream**
**1 can whipped cream**
**2 maraschino cherries with stems**

Prepare each tortilla by frying in hot oil in frying pan. Fry each side over medium heat for about 1 minute or until crispy. Drain on paper towels. Combine cinnamon and sugar in a small bowl. Sprinkle half over both sides of both fried tortillas. Combine remaining half of cinnamon mixture with cornflake crumbs then pour mixture into a plate. Roll a large scoop of ice cream in cornflake crumbs until entire surface is evenly coated. Place coated ice cream on center of cinnamon coated tortilla. Spray whipped cream around the base of ice cream. Spray additional whipped cream on top and finish with a cherry. Serve with honey or chocolate syrup or strawberry syrup on the side for dipping.

**Restaurant Recipe**

# Jack's Roadhouse

**16878 South FM Road 4**
**Santo, TX 76472**
**940-769-2290**
**www.jacksroadhouse.club**
**Find us on Facebook**

Feel at home at Jack's Roadhouse for great food cooked Texas style. Jack's has everything from their very own specialty burgers, specialty chicken sandwiches, catfish, shrimp, chicken-fried hamburger steak and chicken to homemade desserts. They hand batter the onion rings, pickles, jalapeños, and mushrooms. Don't forget to try the Roadhouse Fries, too. There is a great outdoor patio setting where Jack's features live music on Saturday nights. Drop by soon.

**Sunday, Tuesday – Thursday: 11:00 am to 9:00 pm**
**Friday & Saturday: 11:00 am to Midnight**
**(Kitchen closes at 10:00 pm)**

## Roadhouse Rub

**2 pounds brown sugar**

**¾ cup kosher salt**

**4 tablespoons chili powder**

**4 tablespoons cumin**

**1 tablespoon cayenne pepper**

Mix all ingredients together and store in an airtight container. Good on all meats.

**Restaurant Recipe**

## Honey Chipotle Sauce

**28 ounces buffalo sauce**

**1 (7-ounce) can chipotle peppers in adobo sauce, drained**

**1 tablespoon cayenne pepper**

**3¼ (16-ounce) bottles French dressing**

**2 pounds honey**

Place buffalo sauce, chipotle peppers, and cayenne in a blender; purée until peppers are chopped. Pour into a large container; add French dressing and honey. Mix with an immersion blender until fully incorporated.

**Restaurant Recipe**

## Country Corn Casserole

**2 (15-ounce) cans whole-kernel corn, drained**

**1 (10.75-ounce) can cream of mushroom soup**

**½ cup shredded Cheddar cheese**

**1 (8-ounce) container sour cream**

**Black pepper to taste**

**1 cup Durkee onions**

Mix all ingredients, except Durkee onions, and pour into a casserole dish. Bake for 35 minutes at 350°. Top with Durkee onions and bake another 10 minutes.

**Restaurant Recipe**

## Jack's Sauce

**2 ounces roasted red peppers**

**1 (7-ounce) can chipotle peppers in adobo sauce**

**3 green onions, finely chopped**

**3 tablespoons granulated garlic**

**1 teaspoon white pepper**

**½ cup ketchup**

**12 ounces heavy whipping cream**

**5 cups mayonnaise**

Drain juice from roasted red peppers. Combine chipotle peppers, green onions, spices, ketchup and cream in a blender; purée until smooth. Add mayonnaise; continue to purée until creamy.

**Restaurant Recipe**

# M G's Restaurant

### 1721 North Woods Street
### Sherman, TX 75092
### 903-893-9011

For more than 30 years, M G's has been a popular family-friendly diner with a nostalgic 50's atmosphere. The burger patties are cut fresh daily, prepared when you order, and served on homemade buns that are also made fresh daily from Mom's Bakery. M G's pleases every customer with mouthwatering foods and exceptional service. Drive on down on Saturdays for "ALL YOU CAN EAT BURGER DAY" and come back on Sunday for "ALL YOU CAN EAT CHICKEN-FRIED STEAK DAY"—hand battered and fried to perfection. I promise, you won't be disappointed. Come by and see them. It's just a really good burger.

**7 days a week: 10:30 am to 9:00 pm**

## M G's Taco Soup

1 onion, diced
2 pounds hamburger meat
2 (15-ounce) cans pinto beans
1 (15-ounce) can whole-kernel corn
1 (10-ounce) can Rotel tomatoes
2 (14-ounce) cans stewed tomatoes
1 (4-ounce) can chopped green chiles
1 (1-ounce) package dry ranch dressing mix
1 (1.25-ounce) package taco seasoning

Sauté onion in large pot. Add hamburger meat and cook until browned; drain. Combine remaining ingredients in another pot and bring to a boil. Add meat mixture and simmer a few minutes. Serve hot with tortilla chips and cheese in the bowl. This make 1 gallon of soup.

**Restaurant Recipe**

# Something Different by Kay

**706 Lone Star Street**
**Silverton, TX 79257**
**806-823-2063**
**Find us on Facebook**

Something Different by Kay is a small-town family restaurant serving lunch specials Sunday through Friday. Fried catfish, BBQ brisket, and sausage are on the menu Fridays, with all the homemade trimmings including hushpuppies and a different flavor cobbler each week. The menu includes breakfast until 11:00 am (10:30 am on Sundays), handmade burgers, Mexican food, chicken-fried steaks, and several hand-breaded home-cooked meats. Other dishes available include pizza and wings, plus a variety of salads and sandwiches.

**Monday – Saturday: 6:00 am to 9:00 pm**
**Sunday: 8:00 am to 8:00 pm**

## Honey Bun Cake

1 yellow cake mix

⅔ cup oil

½ cup water

½ cup sugar

4 eggs

8 ounces sour cream

½ cup brown sugar

2 teaspoons cinnamon

2 cups powdered sugar

6 tablespoons milk

Combine dry cake mix, oil, water, sugar, eggs and sour cream; mix well. Pour half the batter in a greased 9x13-inch cake pan. In a separate bowl, mix brown sugar and cinnamon. Sprinkle over batter in pan. Top with remaining batter and swirl through with a knife. Bake at 350° for 40 to 45 minutes. Combine powdered sugar and milk. Pour over cake while still warm.

**Restaurant Recipe**

## Homemade Cinnamon Rolls

*Some say these should be called sticky buns, but this is my mom's recipe, and growing up we called them cinnamon rolls. They will always be my favorite cinnamon rolls.*

**Yeast bread dough to make 1 loaf bread**

**½ cup butter, melted**

**¾ cup sugar**

**½ cup pancake syrup (not corn syrup or flavored syrups)**

Allow dough to rise to double in bulk. Roll it out to ¼-inch thickness into a rectangle shape. Spread with melted butter. Sprinkle sugar evenly over dough. Roll up dough from longest side and cut into rolls. Spray a pan with plenty of nonstick cooking spray. Pour syrup into bottom of pan and spread. Place rolls on top of syrup and let rise until double again. Bake at 350° until golden on top. Remove from oven, invert onto tray immediately.

**Restaurant Recipe**

# The Butcher's Block
## Eats and Drinks

**1600 25th Street**
**Snyder, TX 79549**
**325-436-0205**

The Butcher's Block brings big city dining to west Texas. Specializing in steaks and seafood, Chef Jere Cervantez and his team offer distinctive dishes created with the freshest ingredients, excellent service, and a relaxing atmosphere. Everything is homemade and fresh, from the quail and jalapeño appetizer to hand-cut steaks perfectly cooked and well seasoned. A full bar is also available if you enjoy a drink with your meal. Come for lunch or dinner, and order anything on the menu. It's all good at The Butcher's Block.

**Monday – Thursday: 11:00 am to 9:00 pm**
**Friday & Saturday: 11:00 am to 10:00 pm**
**Sunday: 11:30 am to 2:00 pm**

## Deconstructed Cabbage Rolls

1 tablespoon extra virgin olive oil
1½ to 2 pounds lean ground beef
1 large onion, chopped
1 clove garlic, minced
1 small head cabbage, chopped
2 (14-ounce) cans diced tomatoes
1 (8-ounce) can tomato sauce
½ cup water
1 teaspoon ground black pepper
1 teaspoon sea salt

In a large skillet, heat olive oil over medium heat. Add ground beef and onion; cook, stirring frequently and breaking up meat with the spoon, until beef is no longer pink and onion is tender. Add garlic and continue cooking for 1 minute. Add remaining ingredients, and bring to a boil. Cover and simmer 20 to 30 minutes, or until cabbage is tender.

**Local Favorite**

Welcome to
**Howell's Western Cafe**

We Serve Breakfast All Day
Open 7 Days a Week
817-220-7915
Sun - Thurs  6 am - 10 pm
Fri & Sat 6 am - 12 am

*Since May 18th, 1962*

199 West, Springtown, Texas 76082

# Howell's Western Café

**401 West Highway 199**
**Springtown, TX 76082**
**817-220-7915**
**Find us on Facebook**

For the best in Mom and Pop places to eat, do not pass up Howell's Western Café in Springtown. They have been doing business since May 1962, and they know how to do it right. You'll enjoy classics like Matt Dillon sandwich, Cole Younger burger, Calamity Jane's chicken, and even Nemo's seafood. Daily lunch specials are posted on the board and are always a local favorite. At Howell's, your tea glass is always full, and food comes piping hot delivered with a smile by the energetic staff. Metal ceiling tiles and real vintage signs set the mood for great food and outstanding service.

**Sunday – Thursday:**
**6:00 am to 10:00 pm**
**Friday & Saturday:**
**6:00 am to 12:00 am**

## Italian Sausage Skillet

1 pound Italian sausage

2 tablespoons chopped onion

2 cups cooked rice

1½ cups tomatoes

½ cup chili sauce (or ketchup)

In a skillet, fry sausage and onions; drain. Add remaining ingredients, mixing well. Cover with lid; simmer 30 minutes over low heat. Do not remove lid until time is up.

**Local Favorite**

## Buttermilk Waffles

1¾ cups all-purpose flour

1 teaspoon baking powder

1 teaspoon baking soda

½ teaspoon salt

2 cups buttermilk

⅓ cup oil

2 eggs, beaten

In a bowl, mix dry ingredients; set aside. In another bowl, combine wet ingredients. Combine the two mixtures, but do not overmix. Cook in waffle iron.

**Local Favorite**

## Old-Fashioned Tea Cakes

1¾ cups sugar

1 cup Crisco

2 eggs

3 cups all-purpose flour

½ teaspoon baking soda

½ teaspoon salt

1 teaspoon vanilla

Cream sugar and Crisco. Add eggs, one at a time, beating after each. Add flour, soda, salt and vanilla. Mix well. Knead dough on floured surface, roll out, and cut with biscuit cutter. Place tea cakes on a lightly treated baking sheet. Bake at 325° for 8 minutes.

**Local Favorite**

# Alaniz Real Pit BBQ & More

**1204 School Street**
**Stanton, TX 79782**
**432-607-2474**

For seven years, Alaniz Real Pit BBQ & More has served outstanding barbecue. Locals love their slow-smoked ribs and brisket, and the homemade sides are always a favorite. The outside may not be fancy, but once inside, you will be served by a friendly staff that will make you feel right at home. The wonderful aroma of smoking meat greets you right away, and you won't be disappointed when your food arrives tasting even better than it smells. If you are anywhere near Stanton, don't miss a trip to this hometown favorite—Alaniz Real Pit BBQ.

**Monday – Friday:**
**6:00 am to 2:00 pm**
**Thursday & Friday Evenings:**
**5:00 pm to 8:00 pm**
**Saturday: 7:00 am to 11:00 am**

## *Deviled Ham*

**2 cups finely chopped ham**
**¼ cup diced red bell pepper**
**¼ cup diced onion**
**1 large dill pickle, diced**
**1 teaspoon pickle juice**
**1 jalapeño, seeded, stemmed and diced**
**3 tablespoons mayonnaise**
**3 tablespoons prepared yellow mustard**
**Salt and black pepper to taste**

Place all ingredients in a food processor and pulse in spurts until ingredients are blended but not smooth (the goal is to keep some texture). Delicious on a sandwich, crackers, or crostini.

**Local Favorite**

## Armadillo Eggs

4 ounces cream cheese, softened

¼ cup shredded Cheddar cheese

1 garlic clove, minced

1 teaspoon chopped cilantro

¼ teaspoon ground cumin

Salt to taste

6 jalapeños

2 pounds ground (breakfast) sausage

Preheat oven to 375° and coat a baking sheet with nonstick spray. Combine cream cheese, Cheddar cheese, garlic, cilantro and cumin until well blended. Salt to taste. Remove stems from jalapeños and cut in half lengthwise. Remove seeds and cut in half again, horizontally. Fill each jalapeño slice with about 1 teaspoon cream cheese filling. Pat about ⅓ cup sausage into a 3-inch circle. Place one stuffed jalapeño in the center and wrap sausage around until it's completely covered, forming an egg shape. Repeat using all jalapeños. Place on coated baking sheet, about an inch apart. Bake 15 to 20 minutes, or until sausage is cooked through. Delicious served with ranch dressing for dipping. Makes 24 Armadillo Eggs.

**Local Favorite**

## Cantaloupe Ice Cream

2 cups diced ripe cantaloupe

1 (16-ounce) carton half-and-half, divided

1 (8-ounce) carton heavy cream

2 eggs

¾ cup sugar

1 teaspoon vanilla extract

2 tablespoons lemon juice

½ teaspoon cinnamon

½ teaspoon salt

In a blender, purée cantaloupe with ½ cup half-and-half. Pour in a saucepan over medium heat. Add heavy cream and cook just until warm (do not boil). Remove from heat. Beat eggs with sugar, vanilla, lemon juice, cinnamon and salt. Temper egg mixture by adding about ½ cup warm mixture to it, stirring quickly. Then add egg mixture to saucepan. Set burner to medium low and cook, stirring constantly, 5 minutes or until it gets slightly thick (coats the back of your spoon). Cool slightly then refrigerate 4 hours. Freeze and churn according to your ice cream maker's instructions using the remaining half-and-half to reach fill line, if needed.

**Local Favorite**

# Soup & More / Goin' Nuts

**309 West Washington
Stephenville, TX 76401
254-434-4900**
www.facebook.com/soupatthecornerstore

Soup & More is a quaint little restaurant located just off the downtown square in Stephenville. A converted old-time service station houses the soup store where locals and visitors can eat their favorite soup and sandwich. The aroma of fresh baked pies, Belgian sugar waffles, and crêpes fill the dining room. You will also discover a unique candy store—**Goin' Nuts**—where you can pick up cinnamon roasted pecans and almonds along with fresh fudge, all made in-house. Hand-dipped chocolates provide a tasty after-lunch or dinner treat.

**Monday & Tuesday: 11:00 am to 4:00 pm
Wednesday – Friday: 11:00 am to 7:00 pm
Saturday: 11:00 am to 2:00 pm**

## Corn Chowder

4 or 5 potatoes, peeled and diced
1 medium onion, chopped
3 stalks celery, chopped
1 (15-ounce) whole-kernel corn
1 (15-ounce) can cream-style corn
1 (12-ounce) can evaporated milk
2 chicken bouillon cubes
¼ pound Velveeta cheese, cubed

In a large pot over medium heat, cook potatoes in salted water to cover. Drain and set aside. In same pot, sweat onion and celery until softened, about 5 minutes. Add corn, evaporated milk, potatoes, bouillon and cheese. Simmer 15 minutes or until cheese is melted.

**Restaurant Recipe**

## Sister 2 x 4

*This is my sister's recipe and is served on Wednesdays at the restaurant.*

2 pounds ground beef
2 (15-ounce) cans corn
2 (10-ounce) cans Rotel tomatoes
2 (15-ounce) cans Ranch Style Beans
1 small onion, chopped
Salt and pepper to taste

Brown beef; drain. Add remaining ingredients and simmer 15 minutes.

**Restaurant Recipe**

## Gone-All-Day Casserole

1 cup uncooked rice
1 cup chopped celery
1 cup chopped carrots
2 (4-ounce) cans mushrooms, drained
1 large onion, chopped
1 garlic clove, minced
½ cup slivered almonds
3 beef bouillon cubes
2½ teaspoons seasoned salt
2 pounds boneless round steak,
cut into 1-inch cubes
3 cups water

Layer ingredients in a slow cooker in order, starting with rice on the bottom. Cover and cook on low 6 to 8 hours or until rice is tender. Stir before serving.

**Family Favorite**

# Mama Faye's BBQ

**105 North Davis Street**
**Sulphur Springs, TX 75482**
**903-885-0300**
**www.mamafayesbbq.com**

Mama Faye's has been named #1 in the Deep Ellum neighborhood three of the last five years for good reason. Ms. Francine learned how to smoke meats from her mother, Mama Faye, who learned it from her father. The family has been smoking meat this way since 1841, and still does it the same way today. Come enjoy ribs, pulled pork, beef, chicken, and turkey along with amazing sides cooked fresh daily. Enjoy live bands, too, on special occasions.

**Monday – Saturday: 10:00 am to 9:00 pm**
**Sunday: 10:00 am to 4:00 pm**

## Candied Yams

**2 sticks real butter**

**6 large sweet potatoes, peeled, sliced in ½-inch thick rounds**

**3 cups sugar, divided**

**2 tablespoons vanilla extract, divided**

**1 teaspoon lemon extract, divided**

**1½ teaspoons nutmeg**

Melt butter in a large saucepan. Add half of each remaining ingredient: potatoes, sugar, vanilla, lemon extract and nutmeg. Mix well. Add remaining ingredients and mix well. Cover and cook over medium heat until potatoes are soft. Stir often to prevent scorching; do not overcook. Juice should be thick like syrup.

**Family Favorite**

# Bryce's Cafeteria

**2021 Mall Drive • Texarkana, TX 75503**
**903-792-1611 • www.brycescafeteria.com**

Bryce's has served southern-style food made fresh daily since 1931 when Bryce Lawrence, Sr. opened his dream restaurant in downtown Texarkana. The food at Bryce's Cafeteria was a hit from day one, and it quickly became the go-to place for lunch and dinner for Texarkana residents and those traveling through town as well. Sunday lunch at "The Cafeteria" is a Texarkana tradition and local social event. The menu changes twice daily but always has fried chicken, roast beef and gravy, baked fish, mashed potatoes, and fish almondine. Don't forget to try a slice of Bryce's Cafeteria's famous pies— pecan, coconut meringue, apple or chocolate pie are favorites. The strawberry shortcake is a hit, too. In the summer, be sure to get a slice of their signature peach pie made from locally grown peaches. Be sure to stop at Bryce's Cafeteria where they look forward to serving you with a smile.

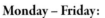

**Monday – Friday:**
**11:00 am to 2:00 pm; 5:00 pm to 8:00 pm**
**Saturday: 11:00 am to 8:00 pm**
**Sunday: 11:00 am to 3:00 pm**

**DRIVE-THRU HOURS:**
**Monday – Saturday: 11:00 am to 8:00 pm**
**Sunday: 11:00 am to 3:00 pm**

## Gourmet Chicken Spaghetti

4 chicken breast halves

8 ounces thin spaghetti

8 tablespoons (1 stick) butter, divided

4 tablespoons all-purpose flour

1 cup heavy cream

1 cup mayonnaise

1 (8-ounce) carton sour cream

1 cup grated Parmesan cheese
plus more for topping

⅛ cup lemon juice

⅓ cup white wine

½ teaspoon garlic powder

½ teaspoon cayenne

1 teaspoon dry mustard

1 teaspoon salt

8 ounces mushrooms, sliced

Paprika

Boil chicken until done in water to cover. Reserve 1 cup chicken stock and debone chicken; set aside. Break spaghetti into thirds and cook in water to cover; drain. Melt 4 tablespoons butter in saucepan; add flour and cook until bubbly. Add cream and reserved chicken stock, stirring and cooking until thick. Add mayonnaise, sour cream, Parmesan, lemon juice, wine and seasonings. Sauté mushrooms in remaining 4 tablespoons butter. Place mushrooms, chicken and spaghetti in 9x13-inch baking dish; stir in sauce. Sprinkle with paprika and additional Parmesan. Bake at 350° for 30 to 40 minutes. Serves 10 to 12.

**Restaurant Recipe**

## Lydia's Cheese Cauliflower

¼ cup chopped green bell pepper

¼ cup butter

¼ cup all-purpose flour

2 cups milk

1 teaspoon salt

1 head cauliflower, cut into flowerets

1 (6-ounce) can mushrooms
(or 6 ounces fresh mushrooms,
cooked in butter)

6 slices American cheese

1 (4-ounce) jar diced pimentos

Paprika

In a saucepan, sauté bell pepper in butter until soft. Add flour and stir to a paste. Combine salt and milk and whisk into bell pepper mixture a cup at a time until blended. Cook until sauce thickens, stirring constantly to prevent burning. (I make this in the microwave in a large Pyrex bowl cooking 6 minutes then testing for thickness and cooking longer, if needed.) Boil cauliflower 5 to 7 minutes in a large pot of water. (Don't overcook as it will continue to soften in oven.) Drain and place in a 9x13-inch pan. Add mushrooms. Add cheese slices, pimento and sauce. Stir very gently. Sprinkle with paprika and bake at 350° for 30 minutes or until warm in center, stirring once. Enjoy.

**Family Favorite**

292 County Road 107
Thurber, TX 76463
254-672-5848
www.thurbernewyorkhill.com
www.facebook.com/NewYorkHill

Named for its historic location atop NY Hill overlooking the town site of Thurber with sweeping views of Palo Pinto and Erath counties, the restaurant was opened in 1989 by Janis & Les Mills, and is proudly owned and operated by three generations of the Mills family, cutting steaks, grinding hamburger, and preparing yeast rolls and cinnamon rolls daily. Enjoy seasonal foliage or resident hummingbirds while choosing from hand-breaded chicken-fried steak, grilled steaks and shrimp, fresh salads and vegetables, or a hearty breakfast featuring hash brown omelets. Afterwards, stretch your legs in the adjacent Thurber historical park or WK Gordon Museum. See you soon.

Sunday – Thursday: 7:30 am to 9:00 pm
Friday & Saturday: 7:30 am to 10:00 pm

## Buttermilk Pie

2 cups sugar

2 heaping tablespoons flour

½ cup butter, melted

1 cup buttermilk

3 eggs, beaten

1 teaspoon vanilla

1 unbaked pie shell

Mix sugar, flour and butter together. Add buttermilk, eggs and vanilla. Mix well until smooth. Pour into pie shell. Bake at 400° for 10 minutes. Lower oven to 350° and bake 30 more minutes. Pie will turn a nice golden brown on top and inserted knife should come out clean.

**Restaurant Recipe**

## Grandma Gordon's Angel Biscuits

1 (.25-ounce) package active dry yeast

⅓ cup warm water

4½ cups sifted all-purpose flour plus ½ cup for rolling dough

1 teaspoon baking soda

3 teaspoons baking powder

3 tablespoons sugar

1 teaspoon salt

2 cups buttermilk

¾ cup vegetable oil

Mix yeast and water in a small bowl and set aside. Mix 4½ cups sifted flour plus remaining dry ingredients; make a well in the center. Pour in buttermilk, oil and yeast; stir until stiff. Spread ½ cup flour on rolling surface. Dump mixture and roll to approximately ¼ inch thick. Use a biscuit cutter or glass to cut. Coat a pan with oil. Rub cut biscuits with oil on both sides from oiled pan. Cook at 350° until lightly brown, about 15 minutes.

**Family Favorite**

# Buck's One Stop Café

**8773 West I-20 (Exit 207)**
**Westbrook, TX 79565**
**325-644-5222**

Buck's Café is found in the small town of Westbrook, out in the oil patch as some say. There's not a lot here, except a lot of good cooking. At Buck's you will enjoy hand-breaded chicken-fried steak, old-fashioned Mexican dinners, hand-battered onion rings or that famous Friday fish. Don't forget Sally's banana pudding; no one else does. Many come from afar to enjoy Sally's cooking, coffee with the farmers and oilfield gossip. Thanksgiving Day is a day of thanks to all their customers, truckers, workers and family—everyone eats together at no charge.

**Monday – Friday:**
**6:00 am to 8:00 pm**

**Saturday & Sunday:**
**6:00 am to 2:00 pm**

### Sally's Banana Pudding

1 (5.1-ounce) box vanilla instant
pudding

1 (14-ounce) can sweetened
condensed milk

3 cups whole milk

8 to 9 bananas, sliced in rounds

1 (8-ounce) carton Cool Whip

2 (12-ounce) boxes vanilla wafers

Mix vanilla pudding and milks together in large bowl until mixed well. Add banana slices. Fold in Cool Whip; mix in the wafers. Pour into 9x13-inch casserole dish. Refrigerate 2 to 4 hours. Enjoy a bowl or two.

**Family Favorite**

# Backroad BBQ

**25646 Highway 377 North**
**Whitesboro, TX 76273**
**903-651-1542**
**Find us on Facebook: Backroad BBQ**

Backroad BBQ is located in the small Texas community of Sandusky, about 7 miles from beautiful Lake Texoma on the Texas and Oklahoma state line. A small roadside barbecue stand, started by the owner's family in 2011, Backroad BBQ has developed a large number of devoted customers and good friends while serving people from Dallas, Texas, to Ardmore, Oklahoma, and many more places. You may visit in route to Lake Texoma for summer fun, but you will keep coming back to pick up more barbecue. Their motto is "To promote our business with good Texas hospitality, good food, and consistent service."

**Open March through October**
**Thursday – Saturday: 11:00 am to 6:00 pm**

## Mema's Tea

2 cups water
1 family-size tea bag
1 cup sugar

Bring water to a boil. Turn burner off and drop in tea bag. Cover with a lid and let steep 20 minutes. Pour into tea pitcher. Add 1 cup sugar and cold water to make 1 gallon tea; mix well.

**Restaurant Recipe**

## Pinto Beans

1 pound dry pinto beans
1 teaspoon salt
2 teaspoons onion powder
2 teaspoons garlic powder
¾ teaspoon coarse black pepper
1 teaspoon Tony Chachere's
Creole seasoning

Rinse beans well. Place in crockpot and cover with water. Cook on low overnight. When done, add spices.

**Restaurant Recipe**

## Peach Cobbler

3 cups peeled and sliced peaches
1 cup water
1½ cups sugar, plus more for crust
1 tablespoon butter,
plus more for crust
2 pie crusts

In a medium saucepan, combine peaches, water, sugar and butter. Bring to a boil. As peaches are boiling cut 1 crust in small squares, as for dumplings. Add to boiling peaches. Boil until peaches are soft. Pour into an 8x8-inch baking dish. Place 2nd crust on top; brush crust with melted butter and sprinkle with sugar. Bake at 350° until golden brown, about 25 minutes.

**Family Favorite**

## Pecan Pie

⅔ cup sugar
⅓ cup butter, melted
½ cup white Karo syrup
½ cup dark Karo syrup
½ teaspoon salt
3 eggs
1 cup pecans
1 pie shell, unbaked

Heat oven to 375°. Beat sugar, butter, syrup, salt and eggs with a beater until mixed. Stir in pecans. Pour into pie shell. Bake 45 to 55 minutes.

**Family Favorite**

# McBride's Steakhouse

**4537 Maplewood Avenue**
**Wichita Falls, TX 76308**
**940-696-0250**
**www.mcbridessteakhouse.net**

Fat McBride's Steakhouse opened in 1992 as one of Wichita Falls' most well-known family-owned establishments, popular for its aged, mesquite-broiled steaks. McBride's Steakhouse changed hands in 2007, but through hard work and dedication, has recently returned to the McBride family. McBride's grandson, Ford Swanson Jr., obtained ownership of the restaurant as of January 1, 2015. He has been following in his grandfather's footsteps since he could walk and plans to continue the McBride legacy of excellence in serving Wichita Falls families as he would his own.

**Sunday – Thursday:**
**11:00 am to 2:00 pm**
**5:00 pm to 9:00 pm**

**Friday:**
**11:00 am to 2:00 pm**
**5:00 pm to 10:00 pm**

**Saturday:**
**11:00 am to 10:00 pm**

## Shrimp Cocktail

**2 lemons, halved, divided**

**10 peppercorns**

**1 teaspoon Zatarain's Liquid
Shrimp Boil**

**½ onion**

**2 celery stalks**

**½ cup carrots**

**1 quart water**

**Pinch salt**

**15 Brown Gulf Shrimp, headless,
shell on (any size will work)**

Place 1½ lemons, peppercorns, shrimp boil, onion, celery, carrots, water and salt in a stockpot (reserve half a lemon for cocktail sauce); bring to a boil. Add shrimp; cook until pink. Prepare an ice bath. Once shrimp are done, drain half the water from stockpot; pour the remaining into ice bath leaving all ingredients and shrimp to cool together. Once shrimp is cool to touch, peel them, but leave tail on. Refrigerate until ready to use.

### Cocktail Sauce:

**½ cup (4 ounces) ketchup**

**¼ cup (2 ounces) prepared horseradish**

**Dash Worcestershire sauce**

Mix ketchup, horseradish, lemon juice (from reserved half lemon) and Worcestershire sauce until well incorporated (if you like it spicier, add more horseradish).

**Restaurant Recipe**

## Grilled Chicken Caesar Wrap

**1 (8-ounce) chicken breast**

**4 ounces romaine hearts**

**2 ounces Caesar dressing**

**2 (12-inch) flour tortillas**

**2 ounces shredded Parmesan cheese**

Grill chicken and slice thinly on bias. Wash romaine and chop; toss with dressing to coat. Warm tortilla in microwave. Pile dressed romaine on tortilla; add chicken and top with cheese. Wrap and cut diagonally. Serve with fresh fruit, chips or soup.

**Restaurant Recipe**

## Steak and Blue Cheese Salad

**8 ounces salad mix (romaine, spinach,
purple cabbage, carrots, radishes)**

**1 (8-ounce) sirloin steak**

**3 cherry tomatoes**

**4 croutons (homemade preferable)**

**2 ounces blue cheese crumbles**

**Blue cheese dressing**

Wash salad mix, dry completely and refrigerate. Fire up grill; cook steak to desired doneness. Let rest 5 to 10 minutes before slicing to retain juices. Place salad mix on chilled plate or bowl; top with sliced steak. Garnish with tomatoes, croutons and crumbles. Serve with dressing on the side.

**Restaurant Recipe**

# Southern REGION

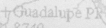

# Camp Verde General Store & Restaurant

**285 Camp Verde Road East**
**Camp Verde, TX 78010**
**830-634-7722**
**www.campverdegeneralstore.com**

Camp Verde, evoking a feeling of stepping back in time to a place full of history, is welcoming and new. This unique store occupies a special setting along the Verde Creek. During the past few years, this General Store has been gradually undergoing a sort of renaissance, introducing a new spirit to this part of the Texas Hill Country. Everywhere you look, there are distinct touches adding to the historical setting of this remarkable venue. Spectacular outdoor patios and a full-service restaurant are surrounded by shade trees that have offered shelter for hundreds of years. Camp Verde will always honor the past and embrace the future.

**Open 7 days a week:**
**Store: 9:00 am to 5:00 pm**
**Restaurant: 11:00 am to 3:00 pm**

## Banana Cream Pie

**6 egg yolks**

**1 cup sugar**

**⅓ cup cornstarch**

**¾ teaspoon salt**

**4½ cups milk**

**3 tablespoons butter**

**3 teaspoons vanilla**

**4 bananas**

**1 pie shell**

**2 cups whipped cream**

In a medium bowl, whisk yolks; set aside. In a saucepan, combine sugar, cornstarch, salt and milk. Cook over medium heat until mixture comes to a rolling boil for one minute. Remove from heat; temper eggs with 1 cup of hot mixture. Pour egg mixture back into saucepan; boil 1 minute. Remove from heat; stir in butter and vanilla. Set aside to cool slightly. Slice 2 bananas into bottom of pie shell, and then add half the cream mixture. Slice remaining 2 bananas; place on top of cream mixture. Pour remaining cream mixture over bananas; top with whipped cream.

**Restaurant Recipe**

## Meatloaf

**2½ pounds ground beef**

**½ cup chopped onions, sautéed in garlic oil**

**2 teaspoons beef base**

**1 egg**

**¾ cup ketchup**

**1 cup panko breadcrumbs**

In large mixing bowl, mix all ingredients until well incorporated. Divide mixture into 3 individual portions and shape into ovals. Brush with additional ketchup. Bake at 375° for 20 to 30 minutes.

**Restaurant Recipe**

# SouthSide BBQ

**16032 South Highway 16
Cherokee, TX 76832
325-622-4444**

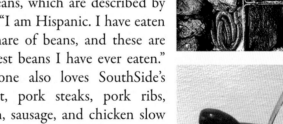

SouthSide BBQ, established November 2011 by Alva and Chris Zulauf, is known for their friendly, down-home atmosphere. SouthSide is the home of Alva's Beans, which are described by one customer in the following way. "I am Hispanic. I have eaten

my share of beans, and these are the best beans I have ever eaten." Everyone also loves SouthSide's brisket, pork steaks, pork ribs, sirloin, sausage, and chicken slow cooked over a bed of mesquite and oak coals. Sandwiches, salads, and stuffed potatoes are also crowd-pleasing favorites while the banana pudding receives rave reviews.

**Friday & Saturday: 11:00 am to 8:00 pm
Sunday: 11:00 to 2:00 pm**

## SouthSide BBQ Brisket Juice

1 (12-ounce) bottle Worcestershire sauce

1 (16-ounce) bottle vinegar

6 ounces Alva's Mix (house seasoning available at SouthSide BBQ)

Add all ingredients to a gallon jug. Fill to top with water. Shake well. Use as a baste when cooking brisket or other meats.

**Restaurant Recipe**

## SouthSide BBQ Banana Pudding

8 cups milk

2 (5.1-ounce) boxes vanilla instant pudding

2 (8-ounce) packages cream cheese, softened

2 teaspoons vanilla

2 (14-ounce) cans sweetened condensed milk

1 (16-ounce) carton Cool Whip

2 (12-ounce) boxes vanilla wafers, crushed

14 to 16 small to medium bananas

Mix milk, pudding mix, cream cheese and vanilla in large bowl for 2 minutes. Stir in sweetened condensed milk. Fold in Cool Whip; add vanilla wafers. Peel bananas, slice right into bowl and mix well.

**Restaurant Recipe**

## SouthSide BBQ Potato Salad

20 pounds baking potatoes

36 eggs, boiled

Salt to taste

11 cups Miracle Whip

½ cup mustard

1 cup sugar

3 tablespoons pepper

3 cups chopped dill pickles

2 large onions

Boil potatoes in water to cover. When cool enough to handle, but still warm, peel and dice into large mixing bowl. Peel boiled eggs; dice into same bowl. Salt to taste and mix well. In another large mixing bowl, add Miracle Whip, mustard, sugar and pepper. Mix well with a whisk. In a food processor, process pickles and onions on chopped cycle till chopped fine. Stir into salad dressing mixture; mix well. Pour over potatoes and eggs; mix well with a large spoon.

**Restaurant Recipe**

# Brewster Street Ice House Grill

**1724 North Tancahua Street • Corpus Christi, TX 78401**
**361-884-2739 • www.brewsterstreet.net**

"Who says you can't have four-star food in a casual environment?" From seared tuna to bountiful burgers and an award-winning chicken-fried steak, Brewster Street Icehouse Grill has some of the best food in Corpus Christi, and you won't pay those full-service restaurant prices. Locally owned and operated and featuring the "Best Texas Country Music" south of Gruene Hall, Brewster Street Ice House Grill is located in the S.E.A. (Sports, Entertainment, and Arts) across from Whataburger Field. Bring your family on game day, stay for a concert or take part in other community events for a family-friendly atmosphere for everyone to enjoy.

**Monday – Sunday:**
**11:00 am to 11:00 pm**

## Fresh Fish Tacos

12 yellow corn tortillas

1 (10-ounce) mahi-mahi fillet,
cut in 6 strips

2 tablespoons butter

1 cup Chef Paul Prudhomme's
blackened seasoning

1½ cups shredded red cabbage

2 avocados, freshly sliced

Warm tortillas. Coat fish with seasoning then sear in butter until coating is crisp and fish is cooked white. Put 3 strips in each tortilla and top with cabbage and avocado. Serves 2. Serve with House Remoulade and Mango Pico de Gallo.

**Restaurant Recipe**

## Mango Pico de Gallo

¼ cup cubed mango

1 jalapeño, diced and deseeded

1 tablespoon freshly chopped cilantro

1 tablespoon diced red onion

Fresh-squeezed lime juice to taste

Place all ingredients in a bowl and mix.

**Restaurant Recipe**

## House Remoulade

1 cup mayonnaise

1 tablespoon ketchup

1 tablespoon Creole mustard

1 teaspoon cayenne pepper

1 tablespoon freshly squeezed
lemon juice

2 teaspoons prepared horseradish

1 teaspoon minced garlic

1 teaspoon Worcestershire sauce

1 teaspoon celery salt

1 teaspoon paprika

Place all ingredients in a bowl; mix well.

**Restaurant Recipe**

## Hello Sunshine Burger

⅓ pound lean ground beef patty

Salt, pepper and a little garlic powder

2 pieces Texas toast

2 crisp bacon strips

1 slice American cheese

1 large egg, fried medium in a Texas-
shaped cookie cutter to shape egg

Season beef patty. Cook to desired temperature. Place on Texas toast and top with bacon, cheese and fried egg. Serve with lettuce, tomato, onion, pickle mayo and mustard on the side. Serves 1.

**Restaurant Recipe**

# Blue Oasis Bar & Grill

**3806 Veterans Boulevard**
**Del Rio, TX 78840**
**(830) 313-7088**
**Find us on Facebook**

Blue Oasis is a family business serving everything from avocado fries to shrimp and rib-eye. With so many handmade recipes, there is something for everyone's palate. The friendly staff makes it a treat to eat at Blue Oasis, which is a sports bar, but is not too loud and not too quiet. Blue Oasis is a great place to eat good food and chit chat with friends and family while watching the games on television. You'll enjoy delicious foods like Mom would make, but you don't have to clean your room.

**Sunday – Thursday: 11:00 am to midnight**
**Friday & Saturday: 11:00 am to 2:00 am**

## Southwest Chicken

1 (6-ounce) chicken breast

1 cup Italian dressing

½ cup rice pilaf, cooked according to package directions

3 onion slices, chopped

½ bell pepper, chopped

½ cup white queso cheese

½ cup poblano Pepper Jack cheese

Bacon bits

¼ avocado, sliced

1 slice Texas toast, grilled

Marinate chicken in Italian dressing. Grill to perfection. Place on a bed of rice pilaf. Grill onions and bell pepper; place on chicken. Melt white queso cheese and poblano Pepper Jack cheese; pour over top. Top with bacon bits and avocado slices. Serve with Texas toast.

**Restaurant Recipe**

## Big Boy Burger

2 (⅓-pound) patties, fresh blend of chuck and brisket

2 sourdough buns, toasted

Onions, sliced and grilled

Jalapeños, sliced and grilled

2 cheese slices

2 slices bacon, cooked

Grill patties until seared, cooked and still juicy. On each bun, layer patty, onion, jalapeños, cheese and bacon.

**Restaurant Recipe**

## Rad's Buffalo Pork Loin Sandwich

1 cup panko breadcrumbs

1 cup all-purpose flour

Dash each: salt and pepper

1 (5-ounce) slice pork loin

Red Hot buffalo wing sauce

Lettuce

Tomato

Deep-fried pickles

Sourdough bun

In a bowl mix breadcrumbs, flour, salt and pepper until well blended. Coat pork loin with mixture. Deep-fry at 350° until cooked through. Coat with Red Hot buffalo wing sauce. Top with lettuce, tomato and pickles on a bun.

**Restaurant Recipe**

# Bill and Rosa's KK Steakhouse

### 7400 County Road 525 • D'Hanis, TX 78850
### 830-363-7230
### Find us on Facebook

Are you looking for an authentic Texas steakhouse experience? Don't miss Bill and Rosa's KK Steakhouse with their rustic saloon exterior, wooden floors, and relics on the walls; you know you are in the right place. This country comfort is combined with frequent live music and a friendly staff that will always make you feel at home. But, the food is the star at Bill and Rosa's. Everyone loves their steaks, burgers, and sandwiches. A particular local favorite is the country-fried steak. Get it with gravy or with cheese and bacon; but unless you are super hungry, get the half-portion, as the "saloon-sized" portions are huge. There is also a great selection of sides, including the famous grilled squash. Great iced tea and homemade pies round out an excellent meal.

**Monday: 8:00 am to 3:00 pm**
**Wednesday & Thursday: 8:00 am to 9:00 pm**
**Friday & Saturday; 8:00 am to 10:00 pm**
**Sunday: 8:00 am to 9:00 pm**

## Rice Soufflé

2 tablespoons butter
½ cup shredded Cheddar cheese
2 cups hot milk
1 cup cooked rice
½ teaspoon salt
2 eggs, beaten
Paprika

Place butter and cheese in a bowl; cover with hot milk and stir to melt. Add rice and salt. Fold in eggs, mixing well. Pour into greased 2-quart casserole. Sprinkle with paprika. Bake at 350° for 30 minutes or until set.

**Local Favorite**

## Pecan Candy

3½ cups sugar
¾ cup whipping cream
1 cup dark Karo corn syrup
Pinch salt
5 cups chopped pecans
½ teaspoon baking soda
1 tablespoon vanilla

Combine sugar, cream, corn syrup and salt in medium saucepan; bring a boil over medium-high heat. Add pecans; cook to soft-ball stage. Remove from heat; stir in baking soda and vanilla. Beat vigorously until thick. Pour onto baking sheet. When cool, cut into 1-inch squares.

**Local Favorite**

## Country Ham Chowder

2 tablespoons butter or margarine
½ cup chopped onion
1 cup diced ham
1 (10.75-ounce) can cream of mushroom soup
1½ cups milk
1 (15-ounce) can cream-style corn
2 medium potatoes, peeled, chopped, and boiled tender
Salt and pepper to taste

Melt butter in a small stockpot over medium heat. Add onion and ham and brown slightly. Add soup and milk and cook until heated through. Add corn, potatoes and seasoning. Continue to cook until thoroughly heated. Cool slightly and serve in warm bowls.

**Local Favorite**

# Meyer's Elgin Smokehouse

**188 Highway 290**
**Elgin, TX 78621**
**512-281-3331**
**www.cuetopiatexas.com**

Meyer's Elgin Smokehouse is a family-owned and operated BBQ restaurant located between Austin and Houston on Highway 290 in Elgin. Since 1998, the Meyer's have used heirloom family recipes to cook and serve traditional Texas barbecue, including St. Louis-style pork ribs, brisket (slow-smoked for 16 hours) and 8 varieties of smoked sausage. That heritage combined with the current generation's creations—East Coast-influenced pulled pork and Tex-Carribean-Fusion pepper-lime chicken—ensures everyone will find something on the menu to their liking.

**Sunday – Thursday: 10:00 am to 8:00 pm**
**Friday & Saturday: 10:00 am to 9:00 pm (Retail Market opens at 8:00 am Saturday)**
**DRIVE THRU:**
**Breakfast: 8:00 am to 10:00 am • BBQ Menu: 10:00 am to close**

## Buddy Meyer's Pinto Beans

*Dad learned to barbecue from his father and his uncle—a bootlegger during Prohibition (but that is another story). This recipe has been handed down at least three generations.*

**1 pound pinto beans, washed**

**1 tablespoon salt**

**1 tablespoon sugar**

**1 tablespoon garlic powder
or granulated garlic**

**1 tablespoon dark chili powder**

**1 tablespoon coarse black pepper**

**4 to 6 ounces bacon or
smoked sausage (optional)**

Add 2 quarts water to a 3-quart pot (or larger). Add washed pinto beans and seasonings. Bring to a boil, then reduce heat to simmer and cover. Add water as needed, keeping beans covered with 2 to 3 inches water while cooking. Do not stir first 30 minutes, then stir every 10 to 15 minutes. Cook 1½ to 2 hours, until beans are tender.

**Suggestion:** Add 4 to 6 ounces chopped bacon or smoked sausage when beans begin to boil.

**Restaurant Recipe**

## Smokehouse Pecan Pie

*This outstanding pie is baked during Thanksgiving and Christmas, to go with the turkey and dressing meal packs sold during the holidays.*

**1 cup sugar**

**3 tablespoons melted butter**

**½ cup dark Karo syrup**

**3 eggs, beaten**

**¾ teaspoon vanilla**

**2 teaspoons cornmeal**

**1½ cups pecan halves**

**1 (9-inch) pie shell, pre-baked**

Preheat oven to 375°. Add sugar, butter, syrup, eggs, vanilla and cornmeal to a mixing bowl. Mix well with whisk. Add pecans and mix until pecans are distributed. Pour into pie shell. Place pie pan on baking sheet to avoid spilling in oven. Place in oven on middle rack. Bake 10 minutes, then turn down oven to 325° and bake another 35 minutes.

**Family Favorite**

# Cabernet Grill
# Texas Wine Country Restaurant

**Cotton Gin Village**
**2805 South State Highway 16 • Fredericksburg, TX 78624**
**830-990-5734 • www.cabernetgrill.com**

The moment you step inside the ivy-covered walls of the Cotton Gin Village in historic Fredericksburg, Texas, you'll be transported to another world. Koi ponds with waterfalls, lush landscaping, romantically outfitted rustic cabins, and unparalleled Texas Hill Country

dining in the highly acclaimed Cabernet Grill-Texas Wine Country Restaurant all await you. It will be an experience you won't soon forget. Come on in and make yourself at home at one of Fredericksburg's most acclaimed bed & breakfasts, and treat yourself to a true Texas Wine Country culinary experience at the highest rated restaurant in Fredericksburg.

**Tuesday – Saturday:**
**5:00 pm to Close**

## Fredericksburg Honey Lavender Peach Crisp

*While the Texas Hill Country is well known for its peaches, it is becoming increasingly known for its lavender farms as well. Both peaches and lavender come into season at the same time and this recipe makes use of both of them in a delicious fashion.*

**6 cups peeled and sliced Fredericksburg peaches**

**1 tablespoon lemon juice**

**¼ cup honey**

**¾ cup all-purpose flour**

**¾ cup rolled oats**

**¼ cup firmly packed brown sugar**

**2 tablespoons lavender sugar\***

**½ teaspoon cinnamon**

**½ cup butter, softened**

**6 scoops vanilla bean ice cream**

Place peaches in a (9-inch) square pan. Sprinkle with lemon juice and then drizzle with honey. In medium bowl, mix together remaining ingredients, except ice cream, using a pastry blender or fork. Sprinkle crumb mixture evenly over peaches. Bake in preheated 350° oven for 35 to 40 minutes or until top is golden brown. Serve warm topped with ice cream. Makes 6 servings.

*Lavender sugar can be found in gourmet shops or online. You can easily make it yourself by combining ½ cup granulated sugar with 2 teaspoons culinary lavender flowers in a spice grinder.

**Restaurant Recipe**

# MoonDog Seaside Eatery

**100 North Casterline Drive**
**Fulton, TX 78358**
**361-729-6200**
**www.moondogseasideeatery-hub.com**
**Find us on Facebook**

MoonDog Seaside Eatery, established in 2004, is located in Fulton Harbor, a small fishing village. From November through March, the community is the home of the largest colony of Whooping Cranes in North America. In the summer, they host thousands of fishermen bay-fishing for redfish, trout, blue crab, flounder, and other seafood. During oyster season, November through April, MoonDog obtains oysters several times a day, serving the freshest oysters on the half shell. MoonDog is also famous for their house recipe crab cakes, fish tacos, fresh fish entrées, and even barbeque, hand-making virtually all of the menu items and several special sauces paired with their dishes.

**7 days a week: 11:00 am to 9:00 pm**

## Beef Wellington Squares

1 sheet puff pastry, thawed

8 ounces baby bell mushrooms, sliced thin

2 tablespoons chopped fresh thyme

1 clove garlic, minced

2 tablespoons olive oil

1 tablespoon butter

½ cup white wine

2 ounces fois gras

8 ounces beef tenderloin, cooked medium rare, sliced thin

Cut puff pastry sheet into 2-inch squares; bake 10 minutes at 375°, until golden brown and flaky. Sauté mushrooms, thyme and garlic in olive oil and butter until tender. Add wine; cook for 1 minute more. Remove from pan. Add fois gras to pan; heat and melt.

To Assemble: Spread fois gras on squares. Put tenderloin slices over fois gras; top with mushroom mixture. Serve.

**Restaurant Recipe**

## Hatch Chile and Cheddar Apple Pie

4 cups peeled and sliced Granny Smith apples

½ cup roasted chopped Hatch chiles

2 tablespoons lemon juice

5 ounces Cheddar cheese, grated

½ cup agave

½ cup brown sugar

½ teaspoon cinnamon

½ teaspoon nutmeg

½ teaspoon salt

½ teaspoon cornstarch

1 (9-inch) unbaked pie shell

In a large bowl, mix apples, chiles, lemon juice, Cheddar cheese and agave. In another bowl, mix dry ingredients thoroughly; add to apple mixture. Pour into pie shell.

### Topping:

½ cup all-purpose flour

½ cup rolled oats

½ cup chopped walnuts or pecans

¼ cup brown sugar

½ cup butter

Combine topping ingredients; crumble on top of pie. Cook on sheet pan in center oven at 375° for 1 hour or until filling bubbles at edge.

**Restaurant Recipe**

# Pecan Street Brewing

**106 East Pecan • Johnson City, TX 78636**
**830-868-2500 • www.pecanstreetbrewing.com**

Pecan Street Brewing is located in Johnson City, in the heart of the Texas Hill Country. Frequented often by locals and tourists, Pecan Street Brewing is known for its handcrafted beers that are brewed on premise and intended to compliment the menu of brick-oven pizzas, fresh salads, burgers, and more. Come sample one of the seasonal brews, or enjoy a year-round favorite in the restaurant, beer garden, or while dancing to one of the many live bands featured on weekends.

**Tuesday – Thursday:**
**11:00 am to 9:00 pm**

**Friday & Saturday:**
**11:00 am to 10:00 pm**

**Sunday: 11:00 am to 9:00 pm**

## Pecan Street Pecan Sweet Chicken-Fried Chicken

**Chicken breasts**

Use your desired number of chicken breasts; this recipe makes enough for a crowd. Rinse chicken and pat dry.

### Seasoned Flour:

**8 cups all-purpose flour**

**2 ounces Cajun seasoning**

**1 ounce kosher salt**

**1 ounce garlic powder**

**Oil for frying**

Combine flour with seasonings. Dip chicken in seasoned flour. Deep-fry until golden brown and cooked through. Top each with 2 ounces honey pecan sauce.

### Honey Pecan Sauce:

**2 cups unsalted butter**

**4 cups honey**

**4 cups toasted chopped pecan pieces**

Melt butter in a small saucepan. Add honey and bring to a boil. Add pecans and mix well. Remove from heat. Stir between servings.

**Restaurant Recipe**

## Portobello Fries

### Beer Batter:

**2½ cups all-purpose flour**

**3 cups beer**

**1½ cups water**

**½ ounce kosher salt**

**1 ounce Cajun seasoning**

**2 cups cornstarch**

**1 ounce garlic powder**

Mix all together and set aside while preparing mushrooms.

### Mushrooms:

**Portobello mushrooms**

Use your desired quantity of mushrooms; this recipes makes a lot. Pull stem off cleaned portobello mushrooms. Slice in strips about ¾ inch wide. Dip in beer batter and fry in hot oil until brown. Serve with dipping sauce.

### Chipotle Ranch Dipping Sauce:

**1 gallon buttermilk**

**1 gallon mayonnaise**

**2 (3.1-ounce) packages dry buttermilk ranch dressing mix**

**3 (7-ounce) cans chipotle peppers in adobo sauce**

Blend well together. Makes 2 gallons; refrigerate leftovers up to 4 days.

**Restaurant Recipe**

# The Friend's Grill

**153 US 83 South**
**Leakey, TX 78873**
**830-232-6301**
**www.thefriendsgrill.com**

The love of good food done right and an ambience of people who care makes The Friend's Grill the best place to eat. From choice-cut rib-eye steak to outstanding BBQ, you will enjoy everything from gourmet to finger-licking foods you ate as a kid growing up. Enjoy live music on Saturday evenings with violinist Dick Walker while eating that rib-eye steak, cut and cooked the way you like it. The Friend's Grill is always there when you need on-site or off-site catering. No matter the time of year, Ms. Ramona is there to serve the people she loves...YOU.

**Tuesday – Saturday: 11:00 am to 9:00 pm**
**Sunday: 11:00 am to 3:00 pm**
*Winter Hours after Labor Day:*
**Wednesday – Saturday: 11:00 am to 9:00 pm**

## Poblano Chicken

**2 chicken breasts**

**½ cup shredded Pepper Jack cheese**

**¼ cup chopped red bell pepper**

Marinate chicken in salt water for 25 minutes. Remove chicken from brine and lightly pound to tenderize. Charbroil 8 minutes (4 minutes each side). Remove chicken to a roasting pan. Pour cream sauce over chicken. Bake at 350° for 35 minutes. When chicken reaches 155°, remove from oven, sprinkle with shredded cheese and garnish with bell pepper. Serve immediately with beans and Mexican rice.

### *White Wine Cream Sauce:*

**5 medium-size poblano peppers**

**1 cup heavy whipping cream**

**¾ cup white wine**

**2 tablespoons all-purpose flour**

**1 teaspoon salt**

**1 teaspoon dried parsley**

Roast poblano peppers on medium hot grill. Remove stem and seeds and process in a food processor until creamy; set aside. In a medium saucepan over medium-high heat, combine whipping cream, wine, flour, salt and parsley. Bring to a boil then reduce heat to low and simmer until thickened. Stir poblanos into sauce.

**Restaurant Recipe**

## Coconut Cloud Cake

*This recipe is simple and wonderfully light and appropriate for any occasion. The icing added to the cake ensures a moist, delicious cake. Use your imagination when serving; for example, caramel or chocolate syrup drizzled on the plate makes an interesting presentation.*

**1 box Duncan Hines Butter Golden cake mix, plus ingredients to prepare per directions**

**1 (15-ounce) tub coconut pecan icing**

**1 cup toasted chopped pecans**

Prepare cake mix according to directions on box. Add icing and pecans. Mix with electric mixer on medium speed for 5 minutes. Cook in a 9x13-inch glass pan. Cool completely. Cover with topping when cool.

### *Whip Cream Topping:*

**2 cups heavy whipping cream**

**¼ cup sugar**

Mix together and top cooled cake. Embellish with additional raw sugar sprinkles on top, if desired.

**Restaurant Recipe**

## Stonewalls Pizza
## Wings & Things

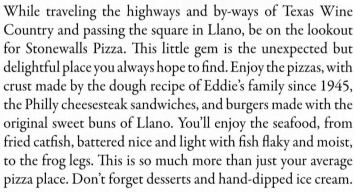

**101 West Main Street**
**Llano, TX 78643**
**325-248-0500**
**Find us on Facebook**

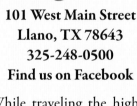

While traveling the highways and by-ways of Texas Wine Country and passing the square in Llano, be on the lookout for Stonewalls Pizza. This little gem is the unexpected but delightful place you always hope to find. Enjoy the pizzas, with crust made by the dough recipe of Eddie's family since 1945, the Philly cheesesteak sandwiches, and burgers made with the original sweet buns of Llano. You'll enjoy the seafood, from fried catfish, battered nice and light with fish flaky and moist, to the frog legs. This is so much more than just your average pizza place. Don't forget desserts and hand-dipped ice cream.

**Monday – Saturday: 10:00 am to 11:00 pm**

## Ham and Noodle Casserole

1 (16-ounce) package wide egg noodles

1½ pounds ground smoked ham

2 eggs

1 cup sour cream

Boil noodles in salted water until done. Drain; rinse with cold water. Place a layer of noodles in buttered casserole dish. Spread a quarter of the ham on noodles. Repeat this process until all ham and noodles are used. Beat together eggs and sour cream. Pour over noodle mixture. Bake at 350° for 30 minutes. Serve hot.

**Restaurant Recipe**

## Creamed Cucumber Salad

2 cucumbers, peeled and sliced

1 tablespoon salt

¼ teaspoon pepper

¼ teaspoon paprika

½ clove garlic, minced

½ teaspoon sugar

3 tablespoons vinegar

2 tablespoons sour cream

½ cup water

Place cucumbers in a bowl. Sprinkle with salt; let stand 1 hour. Squeeze out excess moisture; place in salad bowl. Add seasonings, vinegar, sour cream and water; mix well. Chill before serving.

**Restaurant Recipe**

# Chisholm Trail
# Bar-B-Q

**1323 South Colorado Street**
**Lockhart, TX 78644**
**512-398-6027**

Lockhart is known for great barbecue, and Chisholm Trail Bar-B-Q is the #1 choice because you always get the best barbecue at the best price. The delicious homemade sides include macaroni and cheese, loaded potatoes, coleslaw, fried okra, and more, plus homemade buttermilk biscuits and cornbread. The meat is the star of the show, and you will love Chisholm Trail's brisket, ribs, sliced or chopped beef on a bun, and the local favorite—juicy barbecue sausage. You can even get a beef or fajita taco. So when in Lockhart, go where the locals go for outstanding barbecue. Go to Chisholm Trail Bar-B-Q.

**Daily: 9:00 am to 8:00 pm;**
**Food ready at 11:00 am**

## *Blueberry Cream Muffins*

2 cups all-purpose flour
½ teaspoon baking soda
1 teaspoon baking powder
½ teaspoon salt
1½ cups fresh blueberries
2 large eggs
1 cup sugar
½ cup vegetable oil
½ teaspoon vanilla extract
1 cup (8 ounces) sour cream

Preheat oven to 375°. In medium bowl, sift together flour, baking soda, baking powder and salt. Sprinkle 1 tablespoon flour mixture over blueberries and toss to coat. Set aside. In large bowl, whisk eggs and sugar together until mixture is pale yellow. While whisking, slowly pour in oil. Add vanilla and sour cream and mix well. Fold in remaining flour mixture until just incorporated. Do not overmix. Gently fold in blueberries. Distribute into lined muffin tins. Place muffins in oven and increase temperature to 400°. Bake until muffins are golden brown, 20 to 25 minutes.

**Frances Fielder**
**Family Favorite**

## Broccoli Salad

4 raw broccoli crowns

2 medium tomatoes, diced

1 small onion, diced

1 (4-ounce) can black olives (optional)

1 (8-ounce) bottle ranch dressing

Salt and pepper to taste

Rinse and clean raw broccoli crowns and cut into bite sizes. Add diced tomatoes and onions. Add olives, if desired. Pour ranch dressing over mixture. Add salt and pepper to taste. Mix all together and enjoy.

**Restaurant Recipe**

## Tinker's Chili Stew

1 pound ground beef or chuck

1 small onion, diced

1 (1.25-ounce) packet Taco Bell taco seasoning (or your favorite taco seasoning)

1 teaspoon chili powder

1 (8-ounce) can tomato sauce

½ (10-ounce) can Rotel tomatoes

1 teaspoon salt

½ teaspoon black pepper

½ teaspoon garlic powder

4 medium potatoes, peeled and diced stew size

Put ground meat and diced onions in deep skillet (large enough for all ingredients) and brown. Drain grease. Add remaining ingredients and enough water to cover potatoes; stir. Cook over medium heat, stirring occasionally, until potatoes are soft. Enjoy with cornbread or saltine crackers.

**Family Favorite**

## No Bake Cookies

1 stick butter

2 cups sugar

½ cup milk

1 teaspoon vanilla

2 cups oatmeal

1 cup peanut butter

1 cup chopped nuts

3 tablespoons Hershey's cocoa

Bring butter, sugar and milk to a boil. Boil 2 minutes. Remove from heat. Quickly add remaining ingredients. Stir all together and drop by spoonfuls on wax paper. Cool and eat.

**Family Favorite**
**Grandma "Annie Alexander"**

# Smitty's Market

### 208 South Commerce • Lockhart, TX 78644
### 512-398-9344 • www.smittysmarket.com

Smitty's Market, consistently awarded best of Caldwell County in the meat market, ribs, and sausage categories, and recently 2015 Best Brisket award, offers brisket, shoulder, pork chops, pork ribs, bbq turkey, and two flavors of sausage (regular and jalapeño) prepared and cooked on premises over local post oak wood. Your meats are served on butcher paper with a knife as your eating utensil. If you order beans, potato salad, or coleslaw, they will give you a spoon. Smitty's Market is located in the older historic section of Lockhart right off the "Square." Lockhart has much to offer the traveler looking for small town historic charm mixed with fine casual dining.

**Monday – Friday: 7:00 am to 6:00 pm**
**Saturday: 7:00 am to 6:30 pm**
**Sunday: 9:00 am to 6:30 pm**

# John Fullilove's Rib Roast

*Pairs well with Smitty's Market sausage links.*

**1 (3¼- to 4-pound) 3-bone beef
rib roast**

**Salt and cracked black pepper to taste**

**¼ teaspoon cayenne pepper**

Let the roast come to room temperature.
Combine salt, pepper and cayenne and
sprinkle over roast. Set up your smoker
for indirect heat. Use wood chips,
chucks or logs and keep up a good level
of smoke. Maintain a temperature
between 325° and 350°. (Do not char
the meat!) Smoke 2 hours, rotating it to
expose all sides to heat. Cook, checking
and turning every half hour, until roast
reaches an internal temperature of 130°.
Allow roast to rest 15 minutes before
slicing. Serves 6 to 8 people.

**Family Favorite**

# The Core Coffee House

**13971 Highway 16**
**Medina, TX 78055**
**830-589-3589**
**www.thecoremedina.com**
**thecoreyouth@hctc.net**
**Find us on Facebook:**
**thecorehouseministries**

The heart of The Core Ministry is to be God's house on Main Street. Their mission statement says, "From the outside looking in, we hope you find us hospitable as well as accessible. From the inside looking out, we are blood-bought, God-fearing believers in Jesus Christ who work together, pray together, envision together, and serve one another." Visitors of all ages enjoy the full espresso bar and breakfast menu, plus lunch featuring the long-standing Taco Table with homemade tortillas. Don't miss the fresh-made pizzas and breadsticks drizzled with buttery garlic seasoning. Find us on Facebook at thecorehouseministries.

*"Taste and see that the Lord is good."*
—Psalm 34:8

**Tuesday & Wednesday: 8:00 am to 2:00 pm**
**Thursday & Friday: 8:00 am to 7:00 pm**

The Core

## Heidi's Core Lasagna

*This recipe makes two large pans.*

**1 pound ground sausage**

**1 whole garlic, cloved and crushed**

**1 (1-pound) box lasagna noodles**

**2 eggs, beaten**

**16 ounces ricotta (made from whole milk)**

**92 ounces Thick 'n Chunky Tomato and Garlic Sauce**

**3 to 4 pounds mozzarella cheese, shredded**

Cook sausage. Add garlic and sauté until cooked through. Cook lasagna noodles in boiling water for a minimum of 8 minutes. Mix eggs with ricotta cheese. Set aside. Add sausage to tomato sauce and mix well. Start with a small portion of sauce in the bottom of the pan. Place 3 noodles side by side over sauce. Spread ricotta mixture over noodles. Next spread a layer of tomato and sausage sauce. Then cover sparsely, but evenly, with mozzarella. Repeat process 3 times. (I usually have a bit of sauce left over, but not ricotta. I often have ravioli for the kids to eat with the sauce at this point. It's good!) Bake for an hour at 350°. Serve with garlic bread.

**Restaurant Recipe**

# Williams Creek Trading Company BBQ

### Food Truck Trailer in the Texas Hill Country
### 830-796-1889

Williams Creek Trading Company BBQ is a food trailer cooking traditional Texas barbecue for all occasions, on the street and on location for your private family reunion, wedding or birthday. They have enjoyed a multitude of friends and customers both far and near who have come to eat with them while cooking on the street. Currently you'll find Williams Creek in the Hill Country at the beginning of Texas Ranch Road 337, sometimes referred to as the Three Sister's Ride, or in Medina right beside the legendary "Old Timer." Their goal is to bring quality barbecue to you every time by cooking the old-fashioned way, with wood, and serving only homemade sides and desserts.

**Saturday & Sunday: 11:00 am to 7:00 pm**

## Cider Slaw

1 bunch green onions, chopped
1 cup all-natural sugar
1 cup cider vinegar
¼ cup white wine vinegar
1 teaspoon celery seed
1½ to 2 teaspoons salt
½ teaspoon black pepper
¾ to 1 cup safflower oil
2 heads cabbage, chopped
(or 4 packages precut)

Combine onions, sugar, cider vinegar, wine vinegar, celery seed, salt and pepper in a 4-quart pot and bring to a boil. Add oil and return to rapid boil. Place cabbage in a large bowl and douse with vinegar mixture; stir well; cool to room temperature and refrigerate. It's best the next day. This will feed 40+ people.

**Restaurant Recipe**

## Frijoles Tejanos

4 cups dry pinto beans
(2¼ to 2½ pounds)
3 cloves garlic, chopped
½ tablespoon black pepper
½ teaspoon comino (cumin)
½ teaspoon paprika
Tiniest ever pinch of Mexican oregano
½ bay leaf
1 teaspoon red wine vinegar
1 (14.5-ounce) can diced tomatoes
with green chiles
1 poblano pepper, chopped
3 small red ornamental peppers,
chopped
1 (32-ounce) can chicken stock
12 ounces salt pork
1 large onion, chopped

In an 8-quart slow cooker, add all ingredients. Add water as necessary. Cook on low or warm all night. Do not add salt until totally finished (only if necessary).

**Note:** Cilantro and beer is all that's necessary to make this into Barracho Beans.

**Restaurant Recipe**

# Kloesel's Steakhouse & Bar

**101 East Moore
Moulton, TX 77975
361-596-7323
www.kloesel.com**

Harvey & Diana Kloesel began their restaurant business July 1, 1970. The building has been renovated to include three dining rooms, a bar with a dance floor, including DJ and karaoke music and pool tables, and a front porch with large outside deck seating. A historical marker designates Kloesel's Steakhouse as the site of the Moore Hotel, a landmark built by Samuel Moore, one of the original founders of Moulton. All steaks at Kloesel's are heavy-aged choice and prime beef freshly cut onsite. Kloesel's also serves broiled and fried seafood, pasta, fried chicken, Tex-Mex, burgers, sandwiches, and salads. Homemade plate lunches are served daily. Free wifi.

**Monday: 11:00 am to 2:00 pm
Tuesday – Saturday: 11:00 am to 10:00 pm
Sunday: 11:00 am to 9:00 pm
info@kloesel.com • reservations@kloesel.com**

## Chocolate Praline Pie

⅓ cup brown sugar

⅓ cup margarine

⅓ cup pecan pieces

1 Oreo pie crust

1 (3.5-ounce) package chocolate instant pudding mix, prepared per package directions

Whipped cream for garnish

Boil sugar, margarine and pecans until sugar is dissolved and mixture is bubbly, 2 to 3 minutes. Place in pie shell; cool. Spread pudding over pecan mixture. Refrigerate; top with whipped cream.

**Restaurant Recipe**

## Cajun Sautéed Oysters

2 tablespoons butter

1 tablespoon chopped onion

1 cup sliced fresh mushrooms

1 dozen raw oysters, reserve juice

2 teaspoons chopped garlic

2 teaspoons Cajun seasoning

Dash Cholula hot sauce

2 tablespoons chopped chives

Sauté butter, onion, mushrooms and garlic until tender. Add ¼ cup reserved oyster juice, Cajun seasoning and hot sauce; heat thoroughly. Add oysters and sauté until edges start to curl. Add chives.

**Restaurant Recipe**

## Bread Pudding with Bourbon Sauce

2 eggs

2 tablespoons butter

2 tablespoons vanilla

2 cups milk

2 cups sugar

2 cups cubed bread

⅔ cup chopped pecans

Preheat oven to 325°. Beat eggs; add butter, vanilla and milk. Gradually add sugar and mix thoroughly until sugar is dissolved. Place bread cubes in bottom of a 9-inch round baking dish. Pour liquid over bread, making sure all pieces are fully saturated. Sprinkle pecans over bread and push them down into bread. Bake in oven for 50 to 60 minutes. Serve topped with whiskey sauce. Makes 8 to 10 servings.

*Bourbon Sauce:*

2 cups sugar

2 cups butter

2 cups cream

¼ cup bourbon

Combine ingredients in a saucepan. Stir constantly over low heat until mixture reaches a low rolling boil. Pour a small amount over individual servings of bread pudding.

**Restaurant Recipe**

# Trout Street
# Bar & Grill

**104 West Cotter Avenue
Port Aransas, TX 78373
361-749-7800**

Trout Street Bar & Grill—a south Texas coastal dining restaurant with a Key West vibe— is an upscale, yet casual, dining environment where guests enjoy fresh fish and natural-caught wild gulf shrimp. All the soups and sauces are made in house with only the freshest ingredients available. The chef is persistent in using and featuring only local seafood. Come and enjoy the views from the completely windowed dining room and covered patio. Enjoy the best seafood gumbo this side of New Orleans, hand-cut steaks, farm-raised chicken, and the best pasta dishes ever. If you love sunsets and great cuisine, this is the place for you.

**Sunday – Thursday: 11:00 am to 9:00 pm
Friday & Saturday: 11:00 am to 10:00 pm**

## Tuna Poke

**1 pound yellow fin tuna**

**½ cup small-diced red bell pepper**

**1 bunch green onions, finely chopped**

**1 bunch fresh cilantro, rough chopped**

**Salt and pepper to taste**

**1 small orange, juiced**

**2 limes, juiced**

Cube tuna into a small dice; refrigerate. Combine remaining ingredients, except juices, and mix with tuna; refrigerate. When ready to serve, add juices and taste for seasoning. Serve with fried tortilla chips or Parmesan crisps.

**Restaurant Recipe**

## Vera Cruz Sauce

*This tomato-based sauce is versatile and can be served with fish, chicken or pork—you can even simmer some fresh gulf shrimp in the mixture. We use it on our famous Black Drum Vera Cruz and Chicken Vera Cruz dishes.*

**2 (14.5-ounce) cans diced tomatoes**

**1 red bell pepper, seeded and julienned**

**1 green bell pepper, seeded and julienned**

**1 medium onion, julienned**

**6 button mushrooms, sliced**

**2 cups sliced green stuffed olives**

**1 tablespoon minced fresh garlic**

**1 tablespoon cumin**

**½ tablespoon kosher salt**

**½ tablespoon black pepper**

**1 quart water**

Combine all ingredients in a pot. Cook until bell peppers are tender.

**Restaurant Recipe**

## Chipotle Cream Sauce

**1 quart heavy whipping cream, divided**

**1 (7-ounce) can chipotle peppers in adobo sauce, divided**

**1 tablespoon minced fresh garlic**

**½ tablespoon kosher salt**

**½ cup cornstarch mixed with 1 cup water**

In blender on medium speed, combine ½ quart cream and ¼ cup chipotle peppers with sauce until incorporated. Add to remaining ½ quart cream, garlic and salt in saucepan over medium-high heat; allow to reduce. Add cornstarch mixture to cream sauce and stir until thick enough to coat back of spoon.

**Restaurant Recipe**

# JJ's Little Bay Café

**302 North Business Highway 35**
**Rockport, TX 78382**
**361-729-8787**

Family owned and operated since 2002, JJ's Little Bay Café offers casual family dining with hometown atmosphere and friendly service. You will enjoy both American and authentic Chinese comfort foods all made from scratch. The salad bar is always a favorite, and everyone loves JJ's great selection of burgers. You'll find a complete menu featuring stir-fry dishes, soup, baked potatoes, sandwiches, and much more. And kids—of all ages—enjoy the large fish tank prominently featured in the restaurant. So for local hospitality and great food, don't miss stopping at JJ's Little Bay Café.

**7 days a week: 7:00 am to 3:00 pm**

## Chicken Enchilada Soup

1 whole chicken

2 onions, quartered

2 teaspoons garlic powder

1 tablespoon chicken base

1 tablespoon vegetable oil

1 (28-ounce) can Rotel tomatoes

2 teaspoons cumin

2 teaspoons chili powder

1 teaspoon paprika

Salt to taste

1 (16-ounce) block Velveeta cheese

1 (15-ounce) can black beans, rinsed and drained

Tortilla chips, fried

1 teaspoon sour cream

Boil whole chicken with onions, garlic powder and chicken base until cooked through. Remove chicken and pull meat; reserve broth. Heat vegetable oil in a skillet and sauté Rotel tomatoes until tender. Add to broth in pot. Add cumin, chili powder, paprika and a dash of salt; bring to a boil. Add chicken meat and Velveeta cheese; cook until cheese is melted. Add black beans and heat through. To serve, top soup with fried tortilla chips and sour cream.

**Restaurant Recipe**

## Baked Shrimp Scampi

1 stick butter

4 garlic cloves, chopped

1 tablespoon chopped fresh basil, plus more for garnish

1 tablespoon chopped fresh oregano

1 teaspoon garlic salt

⅓ cup heavy cream

1 pound large raw shrimp, peeled and butterflied, with tails on

Hot cooked rice

Preheat oven to 350°. In a saucepan, melt butter with garlic, basil, oregano and garlic salt, mixing well to combine. Cool to room temperature; add heavy cream and whisk until smooth. Lay shrimp in oven-safe pan with tails up in the air. Pour sauce over shrimp and bake 15 to 20 minutes or until shrimp is pink in color. (Shrimp cooks very fast, so try not to overcook, and remember that they continue to cook out of the oven.) To serve, place rice in center of a platter and position shrimp around it with tails up. Stir remaining sauce and pour over shrimp and rice. Garnish with a small amount of fresh basil to taste.

**Restaurant Recipe**

# Our Family Kitchen

**Grandma's Only Competition.**

## Our Family Kitchen

**324 Highway 35 South**
**Rockport, TX 78382**
**361-727-1111**

"Come to Our Family Kitchen" where we serve you comfort foods from recipes that family and friends have loved for generations. You'll feel at home among family furniture and Great-Grandma Ruby's quilt from the 1930's on the wall. While eating, you can watch the birds at our feeders—hummingbirds, too, in the spring and fall. James makes an amazing omelet, and his liver and onions get rave reviews. Dad (Kevin) is the pro at chicken-fry.

While there, check out the bakery case. You might find Grandma's Texas sheet cake or Mom's giant cookies. Please stop by and you might see Clayton at the door to welcome you.

**Monday – Saturday:**
**7:00 am to 2:00 pm**

**Breakfast served all day**
**Lunch: 11:00 am to 2:00 pm**

## Aunt Kay's Cheesy Grits

2¼ cups quick grits

9 cups boiling water

1½ pounds Velveeta cheese, cubed

6 eggs, beaten

6 dashes Tabasco sauce

Add grits to boiling water. Stir constantly until thickened. Reduce heat to low; add cheese, stirring constantly until melted. Remove from heat. Add eggs; mix well. Stir in Tabasco. Slowly pour mixture into greased 9x13-inch pan, spreading evenly. Bake at 350° for 45 minutes. Cool 15 minutes before serving.

**Restaurant Recipe**

## Grandma Esther's King Ranch Chicken

4 cups cubed cooked chicken breasts

1 (23-ounce) can cream of chicken soup

2 (10-ounce) cans Rotel tomatoes

1 small onion, diced

1 small bell pepper, diced

25 (6-inch) corn tortillas, quartered

Shredded Cheddar cheese

Gently mix chicken, soup, Rotel, onion and bell pepper in a bowl. Layer tortillas, chicken mixture and cheese in 3 layers in lightly greased 9x13-inch pan. Bake at 350° for 45 minutes. Cool 15 minutes.

**Restaurant Recipe**

## Aunt Kimmy's Strawberry Pretzel Salad

2 sticks butter (no substitutes), melted

2 cups crushed pretzel sticks

2 (8-ounce) packages cream cheese, softened

1½ cups sugar

2 cups frozen sliced strawberries

1 (6-ounce) box strawberry Jell-O

2 cups boiling water

Pour butter into 9x13-inch pan. Add crushed pretzels and pat down with a fork to make smooth. Cool until butter is solid (don't skip this step). Combine cream cheese and sugar until smooth. Drop by spoonfuls over cooled pretzels then spread evenly. Spread to edge of pan to seal. Gently press a single layer of sliced strawberries into cream cheese, covering completely. Stir Jell-O into boiling water for 1 to 2 minutes until completely dissolved. Gently pour over strawberries and refrigerate until set.

**Restaurant Recipe**

# Back Door Cafe

**3861 Loop 291 West**
**Roosevelt, TX 76874**
**325-446-2604**
**www.facebook.com/Backdoorcafe2**

Back Door Cafe, a quaint little restaurant located in the small town of Roosevelt in the back half of an old general store, has a menu that caters to country folk. Everyone knows everybody and gathers to discuss daily happenings. Being located in a ranching area of Texas means hunting season is an exciting time with the arrival of the new faces and returning old friends. Back Door Cafe treats everyone like family, making sure you leave fuller than you arrived. Like going home for a visit, you always get coffee and tea for free. So come sit, visit, get a bite to eat, and join the family.

**Monday – Saturday: 8:00 am to 2:30 pm**
**Friday & Saturday: 6:30 pm to 9:30 pm**

**FOOTBALL SEASON:**
**Monday & Thursday: 6:30 pm to 9:30 pm**

**HUNTING SEASON:**
**Sundays: 8:00 am to 2:30 pm**

## Back Door Club with Onion Rings

2 eggs

2 cups milk

2 cups all-purpose flour

½ tablespoon each: pepper, onion powder, garlic powder, seasoned salt

1 large onion, sliced thick and separated into rings

Oil for frying

Mayonnaise

3 slices thin bread, toasted

Kosher pickle slices

Diced tomatoes

Romaine lettuce

2 slices American cheese, separated

Smoked turkey breast slices

Honey ham slices

2 slices hickory bacon, cooked

Mix milk and eggs; set aside. Mix flour and spices. Place onions in egg mix then in flour; repeat. Fry in oil until golden brown. Place mayo on first piece of bread, then pickles, tomatoes, lettuce, 2nd piece of toast, and a slice of cheese. On 3rd piece of toast place turkey, ham, bacon and 2nd slice of cheese. Slice sandwich in quarters cutting diagonally. To ensure it holds together, place a toothpick in the center of each quarter before slicing. After slicing, place sandwich, outside edge down (point up) putting 2 quarters together. Serve with onion rings.

**Restaurant Recipe**

## Lizzy's Pumpkin Cupcakes

1 (15-ounce) can pumpkin purée

4 large eggs

1 teaspoon vanilla extract

¾ cup vegetable oil

2 cups sugar

2 cups all-purpose flour

2 teaspoons baking soda

1 teaspoon baking powder

1 teaspoon salt

1 teaspoon cinnamon

½ cup milk

Preheat oven to 325°. In large bowl, mix pumpkin, eggs, vanilla, oil and sugar; set aside. In separate bowl, mix flour, baking soda, baking powder, salt and cinnamon. Slowly combine mixtures with milk. Spoon ⅓ cup batter into each muffin tin. Bake 18 to 20 minutes. Top with your favorite holiday icing.

**Family Favorite**

# Avocado Cafe
# & Juice Bar

**18771 Farm Market Road 2252 #23**
**San Antonio, TX 78266**
**210-441-8338**
**www.avocadocafesa.com**
**Find us on Facebook**

The Avocado Cafe & Juice Bar is owned and operated by a family who loves spending time with loved ones and enjoying good food. That is what you can expect when you come to this "home" for lunch. Fresh food made to order—with love and consideration of allergies—while you enjoy each other's company. Have a fresh juice made custom to your preferences, indulge in a homemade pastry, and then stroll the local shops after your meal. You'll find something for everyone; vegan, vegetarian, gluten-free, dairy-free, kids, and hungry men.

**Tuesday – Sunday: 11:00 am to 3:00 pm**

## Garlic Soup

3 tablespoons high quality extra virgin olive oil

¼ sweet onion, diced

1 whole head garlic, peeled and diced

1 teaspoon dried thyme

2 bay leaves

3 cups vegetable broth

2 cups water

½ teaspoon finely chopped parsley

2 cups seasoned croutons

1 poached egg per serving

Heat oil in a large pot; add onion and garlic. Sauté over low heat until softened; do not let brown. Add thyme and bay leaves; stir. Add broth and water; adjust broth and water to taste. Boil 5 to 10 minutes. Remove bay leaves. Serve topped with parsley, croutons and a poached egg.

**Restaurant Recipe**

## Guacamole

1 Hass avocado, peeled, pit removed

¼ cup mild citrus salsa

Kosher salt, to taste

½ lemon, juiced

1 orange, juiced

1 tablespoon chopped cilantro

Mix and mash to desired consistency. Enjoy with chips.

**Restaurant Recipe**

# Frank's Restaurant

**11 North Kessler Avenue**
**Schulenburg, TX 78956**
**Exit 674 off I-10/Highway 77**
**979-743-3555**

Deep in the heart of Texas, Frank's Restaurant has been satisfying hungry travelers for more than 85 years. Although our world is ever-changing, Frank's has held on to the comforts of coming home to a great meal. Frank's is not just a restaurant—it's a family. Ginger and Cheryl's motto is: "From our family to yours...enjoy our recipes."

**Daily: 7:00 am to 8:30 pm**

## Frank's Chili

### Slurry:

**3 cups all-purpose flour**

**3 cups water**

Mix flour and water until smooth.

### Chili:

**15 pounds chili meat**

**1 large onion, chopped**

**¼ cup ground comino (cumin)**

**¼ cup salt**

**½ cup granulated garlic**

**4 cups chili powder**

**1½ gallons water**

Brown meat and onion. Drain, if necessary. Add spices and water; cook 20 minutes over medium heat, stirring often. Thicken with slurry. Continue to cook 1½ to 2 hours over low heat.

**Restaurant Recipe**

## Frank's Restaurant Pineapple Banana Bread

**3 cups all-purpose flour**

**2 cups sugar**

**1 teaspoon baking soda**

**1 teaspoon salt**

**1 teaspoon cinnamon**

**1 cup chopped nuts (optional)**

**3 eggs, beaten**

**1½ cups vegetable oil**

**2 cups mashed bananas**

**1 (8-ounce) can crushed pineapple (half drained)**

**2 teaspoons vanilla**

Combine dry ingredients. Stir in nuts, and set aside. In a separate bowl, combine remaining ingredients; add to dry ingredients, stirring just until batter is moistened. Spoon batter into 2 greased and floured 9x5-inch loaf pans. Bake at 350° for 1 hour and 5 minutes, or until a toothpick inserted in center comes out clean. Cool 10 minutes before removing from pan. Makes 2 loaves.

**Restaurant Recipe**

# Brietzke's
# General Store and Cafe

**9015 FM 775**
**Seguin, TX 78155**
**830-914-3288**

If you are interested in an off-the-beaten path journey for great food, don't miss Brietzke's General Store and Café for home-style cooking at its finest. It is well worth the trip when you are rewarded with a genuine hometown atmosphere, freshly cooked food even better than Mama made, and outstanding service.

There is a very well-rounded menu for you to enjoy; some of the local favorites include patty melts, chicken-fried steak sandwiches, fried catfish, and maybe the best burger you've ever eaten. The fries are hand-cut and all the sides are made in-house and served fresh. Whatever you do, save room for dessert—delicious pies, brownies, cobblers, and more—all homemade. Brietzke's is waiting to serve you.

**Tuesday –Thursday: 7:00 am to 9:00 pm**
**Friday: 7:00 am to 10:00 pm**
**Saturday: 7:00 am to 9:00 pm**
**Sunday: 7:30 am to 4:00 pm**

## Baked French Toast Casserole

**1 loaf French bread, sliced**

**8 large eggs**

**2 cups half-and-half**

**1 cup milk**

**¼ cup sugar**

**1 teaspoon vanilla extract**

**¼ teaspoon ground cinnamon**

**¼ teaspoon ground nutmeg**

**Dash salt**

Arrange bread slices in a generously buttered 9x13-inch baking dish. In a large bowl, combine eggs, half-and-half, milk, sugar, vanilla, cinnamon, nutmeg and salt. Beat vigorously with a whisk (or electric mixer) until mixed well. Pour over bread. Cover with foil and refrigerate overnight. The next day, preheat oven to 350°. Spread pecan topping evenly over bread and bake 40 minutes, or until lightly browned.

### Pecan Topping:

**2 sticks butter, softened**

**1 cup packed light brown sugar**

**1 cup chopped pecans**

**2 tablespoons light corn syrup**

**½ teaspoon cinnamon**

**½ teaspoon nutmeg**

Combine all ingredients in a medium bowl and mix well.

**Local Favorite**

## Ham and Bean Soup

**1 tablespoon olive oil**

**1 tablespoon butter, plus more for topping**

**1 small onion, chopped fine**

**2 cloves garlic, chopped fine**

**1½ cups diced ham**

**2 teaspoons chopped fresh thyme**

**2 (15-ounce) cans white beans, drained and rinsed**

**4 cups chicken broth**

**1 bay leaf**

**4 cups chopped fresh collard greens**

**Salt and pepper to taste**

Heat oil and butter in a stockpot over medium heat. Add onion, garlic, ham and thyme in oil and butter; cook, stirring occasionally, until onion is softened, about 4 minutes. Add beans, broth, bay leaf, collards, salt and pepper; simmer, uncovered, stirring occasionally, 20 minutes or longer. Remove bay leaf before serving.

**Local Favorite**

# Ted's Restaurant

**5717 Padre Boulevard**
**South Padre Island, TX 78597**
**956-761-5327**

If you find yourself traveling the island looking for good food, be sure to make Ted's Restaurant your first stop for breakfast and lunch. From the comfy atmosphere in a homey-feeling house to the Texas-size, Texas-style foods, you are sure to enjoy your visit. The food is good, the price is right, and the service always comes with a smile. Local favorites include everything from fajitas and eggs to pecan pancakes. Once you step through the doors, don't be surprised if the next time you come in, you are greeted by name. Everything is cooked to order so it comes out fresh and hot. Ted's is the best bargain on the island.

**7 days a week: 7:00 am to 2:00 pm**

## Angel Biscuits

1 (.25-ounce) package active dry yeast

2 tablespoons warm water

5 cups all-purpose flour

¼ cup sugar

3 teaspoons baking powder

1 teaspoon baking soda

2 teaspoons salt

1 cup shortening

2 cups buttermilk

Dissolve yeast in water. In bowl, combine dry ingredients; cut in shortening. Add yeast and buttermilk; mix well. Store in airtight container in refrigerator until ready to use. Roll in balls, place on baking pan and flatten. Place in warm spot; let rise 30 minutes. Bake at 425° until brown, about 15 minutes.

**Local Favorite**

## Scalloped Potatoes and Tomatoes

1 onion, chopped

1 clove garlic, minced

2 tablespoons butter

1 teaspoon salt

⅛ teaspoon black pepper

¼ teaspoon chopped basil

¼ teaspoon chopped thyme

2 potatoes, sliced

2 tomatoes, cubed

½ cup shredded Parmesan cheese

Sauté onion, garlic and seasonings in butter. Add potatoes and tomatoes; mix to coat. Pour into greased 9x9-inch casserole dish. Top with cheese. Bake at 400° for 40 minutes.

**Local Favorite**

# Brush Country BBQ and Catering

**Highway 281 North**
**Three Rivers, TX 78022**
**361-786-4335**
**www.brushcountryseasoning.com**

Brush Country BBQ is a family owned and operated store and deli. Cooking and catering for more than 30 years, they started cooking at their own cattle sales in the early 1980's. The seasoning is what everyone truly raves about—from Hawaii to Hong Kong. It's even been seen on chef's prep areas in New York. The specialty at Brush Country BBQ is brisket and sausage, and you'll also find pork ribs and chicken. The sides are pinto beans, potato salad, and coleslaw. Burgers and fries are served daily. A customer favorite is the 10-ounce rib-eye steak seasoned generously with the Brush Country Seasoning.

**Daily: 6:00 am to 8:00 pm**

## Chicken–Fried Steak

**2 eggs**

**2 cups milk**

**Round steak, cut into strips**

**4 to 6 cups all-purpose flour**

**2 tablespoons Brush Country Seasoning**

**Vegetable oil for frying**

In a large bowl, combine flour and seasoning. In a separate bowl, whisk together eggs and milk. Dip meat strips into flour mixture, then egg mixture, then back into flour mixture. Set aside on wax paper or a rack until ready to fry. Heat cast-iron skillet with ½ inch oil over medium heat. Carefully lay meat in oil; it should sizzle immediately (if not, turn heat to medium high). Fry meat about 2 minutes per side, until golden brown; place on a paper towel to drain. Reserve pan drippings for gravy.

### Down Home Gravy:

**5 tablespoons flour**

**2 cups milk**

**2 teaspoons Brush Country Seasoning**

Pour excess drippings from skillet used for frying steak, leaving 6 tablespoons. Whisk in flour until smooth and brown. Slowly add milk, stirring so it remains lump free. Add seasoning. Cook until thick like a milkshake. Pour over steak and your favorite mashed potatoes. Serve with a yeast roll. Ultimate comfort food.

**Restaurant Recipe**

BRUSH COUNTRY

BAR-B-QUE & CATERING

FRESH BBQ DAILY

## Ranch Potatoes

*This is a customer favorite and the most requested potato dish at catered events.*

**3 pounds new red potatoes, washed, sliced ¼ inch thick**

**Brush Country Seasoning**

**1½ sticks butter, divided**

**3 cups shredded Cheddar cheese, divided**

Place potatoes in tightly closed foil or tightly covered 9x13-inch casserole dish with enough water to cover potatoes. Bake at 350° for 1½ hours or until done. Drain off water; return a third of potatoes back in dish. Sprinkle with seasoning; top with a third of butter and 1 cup cheese. Repeat 3 times. Cover; place back in oven for 15 minutes.

**Restaurant Recipe**

# Murphy's Steakhouse

### 204 Thomas Street
### Winchester, TX 78945
### 979-242-3433
### www.eatatmurphys.com

Murphy's Steakhouse is located off the beaten path in the quaint little town of Winchester. The building was built in 1913 and still has the original tin ceiling, mortar bricks, and an intriguing mirrored bar. They offer fresh, hand-cut steaks to order, homemade pasta dishes, seafood, burgers, delicious home-cooked lunch specials, a beautiful salad bar, homemade beans, and homemade desserts. Accepts reservations for large parties, special events or dining just for two.

**Tuesday – Saturday: 11:00 am to 9:30 pm**

## *Recipe for Life*

1 cup good thoughts

1 cup consideration for others

1 cup kind deeds

3 cups forgiveness

2 cups well-beaten faults

Tears of joy, sorrow and sympathy,
as many as necessary

4 cups prayer and faith

Mix good thoughts, consideration, kind deeds, forgiveness and well-beaten faults. Add tears of joy, sorrow and sympathy for others. Fold in prayer and faith. Bake well with human kindness. Serve with a smile.

**Family Favorite**

## Firecrackers

1 (1-pound) box unsalted saltine
crackers

1 cup canola oil

1 (1-ounce) package dry ranch
dressing mix

2 tablespoons crushed red pepper
flakes

½ teaspoon garlic powder

Line crackers on ends (like dominoes) in an airtight container. In a small bowl, mix oil, dressing mix, pepper flakes and garlic powder. Stir until all ingredients are well mixed. While stirring, spoon mixture evenly over crackers, like drizzling icing on a cake. Close lid tightly; flip the container over every 5 minutes for 20 minutes. Lightly shake back and forth to make sure all the crackers are coated. Store in airtight container. Will keep for about a week.

**Family Favorite**

## Broccoli Salad

1 head broccoli, chopped

1 cup mayonnaise

½ cup sugar

½ teaspoon salt

½ pound bacon, fried and crumbled

1 cup shredded cheese

Mix all ingredients. Ready to serve.

**Restaurant Recipe**

## Tuscan Rib-Eye Steak

1 (18-ounce) 1½-inch thick bone-in
rib-eye steak

2 teaspoons extra virgin olive oil

4 sprigs fresh rosemary

4 sprigs fresh thyme

2 cloves garlic, peeled and smashed

1¼ teaspoons kosher salt

1 teaspoon fresh lemon juice

¼ teaspoon freshly ground
black pepper

Place steak in a sealable container. Mix olive oil, rosemary, thyme and garlic together; pour over steak to marinate 1 hour or longer. Heat grill pan over medium-high heat. Sprinkle steak evenly with salt. Place on pan and sear 5 minutes without moving. Flip and repeat on other side. Add fresh lemon juice and pepper to taste. Ready to serve.

**Restaurant Recipe**

# Eastern REGION

# Kott's Café

**1059 Highway 90 @ FM 149**
**Anderson, TX 77830**
**936-873-2022**

Family owned since 1985, Kott's Café was started by Bobbie Kott. Bobbie's daughters, Donna and Tina Kott, continue to operate the business after the death of their mother and father, James Kott. Following their family's tradition, all the food in the café is hand-prepared including hand-patted hamburger patties. In a small town, good food can be hard to find, but Kott's Café delivers delicious food and great service for every customer. The Kott family takes pride in this café, and looks forward to serving their community another 30 years.

**Monday – Friday: 6:00 am to 7:00 pm**
**Saturday: 6:00 am to 2:00 pm**

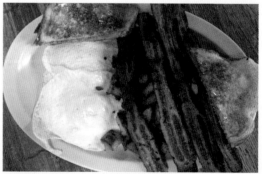

## Coconut Meringue Pie

1 cup sugar
½ teaspoon salt
1 teaspoon vanilla
¼ cup all-purpose flour
3 cups milk
4 egg yolks, beaten (reserve whites)
2 tablespoons butter, melted
1 cup flaked coconut
1 (9-inch) pie shell, baked

In top of double boiler, combine well sugar, salt, vanilla, flour and milk. Cook over medium heat, stirring frequently, until bubbly. Continue cooking and stirring 2 minutes. Pour a little pudding mixture into egg yolks and beat quickly. Add egg yolk mixture into pudding mixture and cook, stirring constantly 2 minutes or until mixture thickens. Remove from heat. Add butter and coconut; mix well. Cool slightly then pour into pie shell. Top with meringue.

### Meringue:

4 egg whites (reserved from filling)
Dash each: salt and vanilla
½ cup sugar

Beat egg whites with electric mixer until foamy. Add salt and vanilla while beating. Add sugar, 1 tablespoon at a time, beating constantly until stiff peaks form. Pile on top of filling and spread to edges. Bake at 350° for 14 minutes or until brown. Cool before cutting. Enjoy.

**Restaurant Recipe**

## Smothered Steak

2 pounds tenderized round steak, cut into serving-size pieces
Salt and pepper to taste
Flour for dredging
2 medium onions, sliced
Oil for frying

Season steak with salt and pepper; dredge in flour. Fry in hot oil until brown. Remove meat from fryer and place in baking dish. Sprinkle with flour. Place onions on top. Add water to cover steak and onions and bake at 350° for 1½ hours.

**Restaurant Recipe**

# Smithhart's Texas Grill

**2440 North Velasco Street**
**Angleton, TX 77515**
**979-848-1320**

Smithhart's Texas Grill is the place to go for good home-cooked foods like Mama used to make. Everything is cooked in-house. From chicken-fried steak, oyster platters, and chicken-stuffed avocados to alligator nuggets, homemade soups, and avocado-stuffed shrimp, you can't go wrong eating at Smithhart's. Good comfort foods, reasonably priced, and healthy portions served by a friendly staff is what you will get. This is a place that makes you smile, and you can't wait until it's time to eat again so you can go to Smithhart's.

**Sunday – Wednesday:**
**11:00 am to 9:00 pm**
**Thursday – Saturday:**
**11:00 am to 10:00 pm**

## Beef Potato Croquettes

**1 pound lean ground beef**

**2 cups grated potatoes**

**¼ cup minced onions**

**1½ teaspoons salt**

**¼ teaspoon pepper**

**Oil for frying**

In a bowl, combine all ingredients. Mix well. Form into 5 croquettes. Fry each side 10 minutes over medium-low heat.

**Local Favorite**

## Creole Beans

**1 cup chopped onions**

**⅔ cup chopped green bell pepper**

**⅔ cup chopped celery**

**2 tablespoons butter**

**1½ teaspoons salt**

**¼ teaspoon pepper**

**2 cups diced tomatoes**

**2 cups green beans**

Sauté onions, bell pepper and celery in butter until tender. Add remaining ingredients. Cook over low heat for 20 minutes.

**Local Favorite**

## Pirate Stew

**1 pound ground beef**

**½ cup chopped onion**

**½ cup chopped celery**

**1 (8-ounce) can tomato sauce**

**1 cup water**

**2 cups peeled and cubed potatoes**

**1 (15-ounce) can red kidney beans**

**⅓ cup rice**

**¼ teaspoon salt**

**¼ teaspoon pepper**

In a saucepan, cook meat, onion and celery until meat is cooked through. Add remaining ingredients. Cover and simmer 35 minutes.

**Local Favorite**

# The Oasis
# on Lake Travis

**6550 Comanche Trail**
**Austin, TX 78732**
**512-266-2442**
**www.oasis-austin.com**
**Find us on Facebook**

Located 450 feet above beautiful Lake Travis, every seat at The Oasis has the perfect view. With casual lakeside dining, two live entertainment venues, and a completely reconstructed menu, The Oasis is celebrating 30 years with style. The once small hamburger joint on the lake in 1982, has now become an Austin landmark, earning the nickname "Sunset Capital of Texas." The OASIS is now bigger and better than ever, with year-round exciting activities, events, and live entertainment. The Oasis is Austin's best destination for family and friends. No trip to The Oasis would be complete without a visit to the Oasis Gift Shop. Buy an Oasis t-shirt or a one-of-a-kind gift made by local Austin artists as a souvenir to remember your visit.

**Open everyday at 11:30 am**
**Closing times vary between 8:00 pm & 11:00 pm**
**depending on day, weather & season**
**See our website: www.oasis-austin.com**

## Enchilada Chicken

5 pounds chicken thighs

32 ounces water

2 bay leaves

2 tablespoons black pepper

2 tablespoons kosher salt

3 tablespoons granulated garlic

1 jalapeño, minced

¾ cup chopped yellow onion

1 bunch cilantro, chopped

Combine all ingredients, except cilantro, in roasting pan. Cook 1½ hours at 350°; remove from oven. Place in smoker at 250° another hour until cooked through. Drain liquid, removing bay leaves (reserve for chicken stock). Shred chicken. Add cilantro and mix thoroughly.

**Restaurant Recipe**

## Crawfish Cream Sauce

1 pound bacon, chopped

1 tablespoon black pepper

¼ cup vegetable oil

2 quarts milk

1 quart heavy cream

2 quarts plus ½ cup water, divided

3 ounces lobster base

5 ounces seafood base

2 cups chopped garlic

¼ tablespoon smoked paprika

1 cup cornstarch

1 pound crawfish tails, rough chopped

¼ cup finely chopped scallions

In a large saucepan, fry bacon with black pepper in oil over medium-high heat until bacon is crisp. Add milk, cream, 2 quarts water, lobster base and seafood base; cook to scalding. Add garlic and paprika; cook 10 minutes, stirring constantly. Thicken with cornstarch mixed with ½ cup water. Turn heat to low; add crawfish and scallions. Simmer 10 minutes.

**Restaurant Recipe**

# Wholly Cow Burgers

**3010 South Lamar Boulevard**
**Austin, TX 78704**
**512- 394-8156**
**www.whollycowburgers.com**

Stop by Wholly Cow Burgers and try their local grass-fed beef burgers, Philly cheesesteaks, reubens, chicken, chili, and more. The menu features local and organically pasture-raised hormone- and chemical-free, grass-fed beef paired with locally grown organic produce when in season. You'll discover many gluten-free and paleo options. The Zen Food Market offers many craft beer selections. Breakfast is served daily. Wholly Cow Burgers has received many accolades, including *Austin Chronicle*'s Best of Austin, and Top 7 Best Grilled Cheese in Texas; as well as **Top 5 Chef-Recommended Burger Joints in the United States** as listed by *Huffington Post* and *Yahoo*.

**Monday – Thursday: 7:00 am to 9:30 pm**
**Friday & Saturday: 7:00 am to 10:00 pm**
**Sunday: 10:30 am to 8:30 pm**

## Green Chile, White Bean and Chicken Soup

**2 (1-pound) packages dry Great Northern beans**
**1 tablespoon olive or vegetable oil**
**1 cup coarsely chopped onions**
**2 teaspoons finely chopped garlic**
**1 tablespoon ground cumin**
**Salt to taste**
**⅛ teaspoon ground red pepper**
**2 pounds boneless chicken breasts, cut into ½-inch pieces**
**9 ounces chopped green chiles**
**2 cups chicken broth**

Cook dry beans in water to cover in slow cooker set to low for 6 to 8 hours (overnight) or until done; set aside. In Dutch oven, heat oil over medium-high heat. Add onions and garlic; cook 4 to 5 minutes, stirring frequently, until onions are softened. Stir in cumin, salt, red pepper and chicken; cook 6 to 7 minutes, stirring occasionally, until chicken is cooked. Stir in beans, chiles and broth; heat to boiling. Reduce to medium-low heat. Cover; cook 20 to 25 minutes, stirring occasionally.

**Restaurant Recipe**

## Fit Cross Burger – Paleo

**2 (4-inch) portobello mushroom caps**

**¼ to ⅓ pound grass-fed beef patty**

**2 strips gluten- and nitrate-free bacon**

**2 teaspoons finely diced onion**

**Green leaf lettuce**

**2 slices fresh tomatoes**

**Mustard (natural or whole grain)**

Grill mushroom caps, beef patty, bacon and onion. Build the burger with all the vegetables and mustard using mushroom caps as the bun. Best served with fresh, hand-cut sweet potato fries.

**Restaurant Recipe**

## Mini Apple Wholly Cow Pie

**2 apples, peeled and chopped**

**¼ cup sugar**

**¼ teaspoon cinnamon**

**2 pie crusts**

**Oil for frying**

In a pot, cook apples down over very low heat with sugar and cinnamon; mash up, leaving chunks. Roll out pie crust on lightly floured board. Using a 3-inch cookie cutter, cut out 7 circles. Place a scant teaspoon cooked apples in middle of each round. Using very cold water and your fingers, wet all around pie edge. Fold over, crimp edges with fork and make a slit in top. Put a little oil in a hot cast-iron skillet; place pies in skillet. Cook 2 to 3 minutes each side. Remove to a wire rack with paper towels to drain.

### Icing:

**1 teaspoon softened butter**

**1 cup powdered sugar**

**½ teaspoon vanilla**

**1 to 3 tablespoons milk**

Whip all ingredients with a fork; glaze pies while warm.

**Restaurant Recipe**

# The Rosebud Eatery & Country Store

**7212 North Highway 317**
**Belton, TX 76513**
**254-780-5511**
**www.rosebudeatery.net**
**Find us on Facebook**

The Rosebud Eatery & Country Store is a comfortable, family-friendly establishment that offers great home-style meals prepared by a professional Chef and served by a friendly staff. Daily lunch specials, soups, quiche, sandwiches, salads, and desserts are on the menu. Casseroles and baked goods to-go are also popular. Most produce used is provided by local farmers. Local vendors, including the owners, sell a variety of items in the country store, such as jellies, dip and soup mixes, pickles, hand-crafted items, crosses, aprons, lotions, soaps, jewelry, and much more.

**Monday – Wednesday: 10:00 am to 3:00 pm**
**Thursday – Friday: 10:00 am to 6:00 pm**

## Pot Liquor Soup

2 to 3 pounds fresh kale, cabbage, and/or collard greens (or a mixture)

2 tablespoons oil

1 large onion, chopped

1 clove garlic, minced

2 stalks celery, chopped

½ cup grated carrots

¾ pound smoked ham hocks

1½ to 2 pounds ham steak, chopped

6 red potatoes, cut into chunks

1 tablespoon white vinegar

Water or stock

2 (15.8-ounce) cans field peas, rinsed and drained

2 teaspoons Chef Ellen's Seasoning Salt

1 teaspoon Tony Chachere's Creole seasoning

Salt and pepper to taste

Remove stems and discolored spots from greens and discard; rinse well with cold water. Drain; tear into small pieces. In a Dutch oven, add oil, onion, carrots and celery; cook over medium-high heat until browned and tender (6 to 8 minutes); add garlic. Stir in greens, ham hocks, ham steak, potatoes, vinegar and water or stock to cover. Bring to a boil. Reduce heat; simmer 30 minutes, stirring occasionally. Remove meat from ham hocks, return meat to soup; discard bone. Add peas and seasonings. Simmer 10 to 15 minutes. Potatoes will help thicken the soup.

**Restaurant Recipe**

## Savory Apple Cheddar Pecan Muffins

¼ cup vegetable oil

1⅓ cups milk

2 eggs

1 large Granny Smith apple, peeled, cored, diced

½ cup shredded Cheddar cheese

4 cups biscuit mix

½ cup pecan pieces, toasted

Preheat oven to 400°. Mix oil, milk and eggs. Add apple, cheese and pecans. Stir in biscuit mix, just until moist. Bake in lined or greased muffin tins 15 minutes.

**Restaurant Recipe**

## Shepherd's Pie

6 to 7 cups chopped vegetables (such as celery, carrots, onions, sweet potatoes, squash, green beans or peas)

2 to 3 cups cooked pork butt (or roast beef ), shredded or chopped

3 to 4 cups brown gravy or white sauce

6 cups mashed potatoes

Cook vegetables in water in stockpot; season to taste. Drain well. Combine meat and gravy; fold into vegetables until well coated. Pour into 9x13-inch pan; top with mashed potatoes. Bake at 350° for 30 minutes or until gravy is thick and bubbly.

**Restaurant Recipe**

# C&J Barbeque

**1010 South Texas Avenue**
**Bryan, TX 77803**
**979- 822-6033**
**www.cjbbq.com**

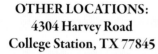

**OTHER LOCATIONS:**
**4304 Harvey Road**
**College Station, TX 77845**

**105 Southwest Parkway**
**College Station, TX 77840**

C&J Barbeque has three locations in Bryan/College Station, Texas—home to Texas A&M University and the Fighting Aggies. The original store opened in 1981, and since then, C&J Barbeque has grown in popularity. For the last 15 years, the citizens of both cities have voted C&J Barbeque as the "Best Barbeque in the Brazos Valley." The restaurants are all set up deli/cafeteria style so you can see your food and order what you want. From a sandwich to as many pounds of meat and sides as you need, C&J will provide plenty of barbeque for any event.

The "Ranch Potato" recipe is the bestselling side dish, and the one everyone wants on deliveries and catering. Visit our website at cjbbq.com to learn more about us. Enjoy!

**Monday – Thursday: 10:30 am to 8:30 pm**
**Friday & Saturday: 10:30 am to 9:00 pm**
**Sunday: 11:00 am to 3:00 pm**

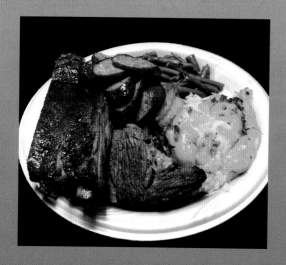

## Ranch Potatoes

1 (5-pound) bag Idaho or russet potatoes

2 to 3 cups ranch dressing

3½ cups shredded Cheddar cheese, divided

1 teaspoon garlic salt

1 teaspoon pepper

1 (1-pound) package bacon, cooked and crumbled, divided

1 to 2 tablespoons dried parsley

Wash potatoes. Slice into ¼-inch-thick slices. Place potatoes in a large pot; cover with water. Bring to a boil over high heat; cook another 20 to 25 minutes or until fork-tender. Heat oven to 350°. Drain potatoes and place in a large mixing bowl. Mash potatoes with dressing, 3 cups cheese, garlic salt and pepper. Use a potato masher or large spoon. (You don't want to use a mixer, potatoes should still have some texture.) If potatoes seem dry, add more ranch dressing. Add two-thirds of the crumbled bacon. Mix and taste. Add more garlic salt and pepper as needed to your liking. Spread in a 9x13-inch casserole dish. Bake at 350° for 10 minutes. Remove from oven; top with remaining cheese, bacon and parsley. Return to oven; bake another 5 to 10 minutes or until cheese has melted.

**Restaurant Recipe**

# J. Cody's Steaks & BBQ

### 3610 South College Avenue • Bryan, TX 77801
### 979-846-2639 • www.jcodys.com

J. Cody's Steaks & BBQ in Bryan is a little different than most steak and barbecue eateries, serving up both tender juicy rib-eyes and mouthwatering barbecue. There's no secret to J. Cody's great tastes. They use a little bit of salt, pepper, and garlic, and grill with a whole lot of Texas-grown mesquite on an open fire and smokes the barbecue with all mesquite. J. Cody's is also known for its vegetable buffet with lots of down-to-earth home cooking and simple recipes, with the corn casserole being the most popular item in the restaurant (aka Cody corn, crack corn, and funeral corn).

**Monday – Thursday: 11:00 am to 9:00 pm**
**Friday & Saturday: 11:00 am to 9:30 pm**
**Sunday: 11:00 am to 3:00 pm**

## Beef Stew

2 to 3 pounds beef, cubed

2 (14.5-ounce) cans diced tomatoes

1 tablespoon black pepper

4 stalks celery, diced

1 onion, diced

½ pound carrots, cut into
bite-size pieces

1 pound potatoes, cut into
bite-size pieces

1 (15-ounce) can whole-kernel corn

2 (14.5-ounce) cans green beans

3 tablespoons salt

Place beef, diced tomatoes, celery, onion and pepper in pot. Cover with ample water and bring to a boil. Simmer till meat is tender (approximately 1½ hours). After meat has become tender, add carrots, potatoes, corn, green beans and salt. It is not necessary to drain canned veggies. Return to a boil. Simmer till potatoes and carrots are tender (approximately 30 minutes). Serve with cornbread. Great for cold winter days.

**Family Favorite & Catering**

## Okra and Tomatoes

*Mmmm good. And a healthy option, too.*

½ to 1 onion, diced

1 small bell pepper, diced

2 quarts fresh okra, diced ⅜ to ½ inch

2 (14.5-ounce) cans diced tomatoes

1 tablespoon salt

½ teaspoon pepper

1 cup water

Mix all ingredients in large pot and bring to a boil. Turn heat down to a simmer and cover pot. Simmer 30 minutes.

**Restaurant Recipe**

## Carol's Garden Mix

1 large potato, cut into ¼ inch wedges

1 large onion, cut into small wedges,
break up layers

3 medium squash, sliced ¼ inch or less

4 cups diced fresh okra (⅜ to ½ inch)

2 cups milk

2 cups cornmeal

1 cup all-purpose flour

Oil

Salt and pepper to taste

Moisten veggies with milk in large bowl. Add cornmeal and flour; mix to coat vegetables. Fry in pan in oil to a golden brown turning occasionally. While frying, break up veggies. Season to taste. Serve with ranch dressing, if desired.

**Restaurant Recipe**

# STAGECOACH DELI

**420 East Commerce Street**
**Buffalo, TX 75831**
**903-322-1700**
**www.stagecoachdeli.com**

Stagecoach Deli is about more than just the average lunch—it is a destination restaurant serving good food, not fast food. Step into the 1800's as you enter the "saloon style" dining area. Buck up to the bar to get some good eats to go or sit a spell and enjoy some good old-fashioned customer service. Fill up on homemade soup and sandwiches or have a real salad that will get you most of your "five a day." The soups and spreads are made on-site. Save room for dessert. Don't miss Wednesday—the only day they serve crawfish bisque. Get there early or call ahead to reserve a bowl because it goes fast.

**SUMMER HOURS:**
**February 1 thru October 31**
**Monday – Friday: 10:30 am to 3:00 pm**
**Saturday: 11:00 am to 3:00 pm**

**WINTER HOURS:**
**November 1 to January 30**
**Monday – Friday: 10:30 am to 2:00 pm**

## Chicken Tortilla Soup

1 pound chicken

3 stalks celery

1 onion

3 carrots, shredded

2 bunches cilantro, chopped

⅓ cup Tone's chicken base

1 (28-ounce) can diced tomatoes

1 (15-ounce) can whole-kernel corn,
do not drain

1 (15-ounce) can black beans,
drained, rinsed

2 teaspoons garlic powder

1 teaspoon pepper

1 teaspoon cumin

½ to 1 teaspoon cayenne

Tony's Chachere's Creole seasoning
to taste

1 cup shredded Cheddar cheese

1 bag tortilla chips

Cook chicken in salted water to cover until cooked through. Remove chicken, shred and set aside. Measure stock from pot and add water to equal ¾ gallon. Heat to a low boil. While stock comes to a boil, chop vegetables in a food processor. Add chicken base and vegetables to pot. Simmer 15 minutes or until tender. Add remaining ingredients, including chicken, except cheese and chips. Heat through. Top individual servings with cheese and tortilla chips.

**Restaurant Recipe**

## Caramelized Pecans

2 egg whites, beaten

1 teaspoon salt

1 cup sugar

1 pound pecan halves

Beat egg whites. Add salt and sugar; mix well. Fold in pecans. Spread on cookie sheet lined with parchment paper. Bake at 275° for 1 hour. Stir frequently. Serve on your favorite dessert or salad. Or enjoy just as they are.

**Restaurant Recipe**

## Pasta Salad

1 (12-ounce) package tri-color rotini

4 ounces cheese and spinach tortellini

2 ounces basil pesto

3⅓ ounces chopped green olives

4¼ ounces chopped black olives

1 or 2 sundried tomatoes, chopped
(or tomato pesto)

1 (8-ounce) bottle Italian dressing

Cook pasta as directed until al dente (firm to the bite). Drain; set aside. In a large bowl, combine all other ingredients except Italian dressing. Toss in pasta. Coat with Italian dressing until drenched. Store in refrigerator.

**Restaurant Recipe**

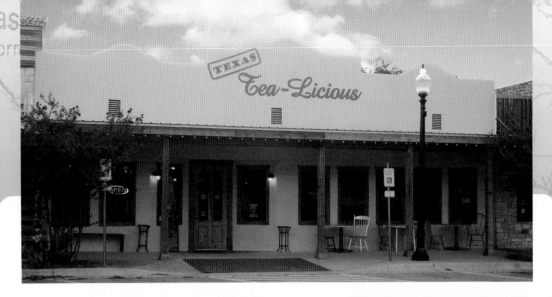

# Texas Tea-Licious

**216 South Main Street • Burnet, TX 78611**
**512-56-7636 • www.txtealicious.com**

Texas Tea-Licious on Historic Burnet Town Square is the place to be for delicious food and fun entertainment. Drop by and you'll see why they recently won honors for "best steaks," "best burgers," "best desserts," and "best venue." Local favorites include bourbon chicken,

hand-cut rib-eye, chicken & dumplings, and chicken pot pie. You will enjoy everything from Cowboy Queso to the jalapeño burger, homemade meatloaf to their famous PEACH TEA, along with outstanding beer and wine selections. Live music and other fun events are scheduled for most nights. Be sure to visit the Food Emporium for an assortment of gourmet and specialty items that will amaze you. Not only is the food amazing, but so are the surprises that await you in the Food Emporium. Visit with Trace and the gang for an awe-inspiring trip back in time when people really cared about you and served you the best.

**Monday – Thursday: 11:00 am to 8:00 pm**
**Friday & Saturday: 11:00 am to 9:00 pm**

# TEXAS Tea-Licious

## A GREAT PLACE TO HANG YOUR HAT & GRAB SOME GRUB!

# BUTTERMILK'S
## scratch cooking on the square

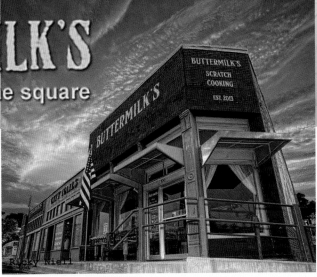

**100 West Dallas Street**
**Canton, TX 75103**
**903-567-3287**
**www.buttermilkscanton.com**

Take a step back in time to when life was a little "more simpler" and food was created with passion. Imagine hand-breaded chicken-fried steak with fried green tomatoes, and finishing the meal with homemade buttermilk chess pie. Back then, life was meant to be enjoyed, and that philosophy is followed today at Buttermilk's. So stop by Buttermilk's and experience comfort food made the old-fashioned way.

**Monday – Thursday: 11:00 am to 8:00 pm**
**Friday & Saturday: 11:00 am to 9:00 pm**

## Chicken Salad

1 whole rotisserie chicken,
pulled from bone

1 cup mayonnaise (more, if desired)

½ cup chopped pecans

½ cup sweetened dried cranberries

¼ cup pineapple tidbits

1 teaspoon apple cider vinegar

½ teaspoon black pepper

½ teaspoon salt

Combine all ingredients, and mix well. Enjoy on crackers or over a nice piece of sourdough bread.

**Restaurant Recipe**

## Chocolate Pecan Chess Pie

¾ cup chopped pecans

1 (9-inch) pie shell, unbaked
(we prefer made from lard)

2 tablespoons flour

¼ teaspoon salt

2 tablespoons cornmeal

¼ cup cocoa powder

½ cup butter, softened

2 cups sugar

2 teaspoons vanilla

½ teaspoon vinegar

3 eggs

1 cup buttermilk

Sprinkle pecans in pie shell. Sift flour, salt, cornmeal and cocoa together. Cream butter in a mixing bowl; slowly add sugar. Stir in vanilla, vinegar and eggs, one at a time. Slowly mix in buttermilk. Add liquid mixture to dry ingredients and mix well. Pour into pie shell and bake at 350° for 1 hour.

**Restaurant Recipe**

## Fried Green Tomatoes

2 cups all-purpose flour

Dash onion powder

2 teaspoons Lawry's Seasoned Salt

2 cups buttermilk

6 green tomatoes, sliced ¼ inch thick

Mix flour, onion powder and seasoned salt in a bowl. Pour buttermilk in a separate small bowl. Dip tomatoes in flour mixture, then dip in buttermilk, then back in flour mixture. Slowly place in hot frying pan with oil of your choice (preferably peanut). Fry on each side till GBD (Golden Brown and Delicious).

**Restaurant Recipe**

# Bunkhouse Barbeque

**1003 South Avenue G • Clifton, TX 76634**
**254-675-8409 • Find us on Facebook**

After competing in cook-offs for several years, Ricky and Pam Countryman opened Bunkhouse Barbeque March 1, 1999. The residents of Clifton welcomed them with open arms and a hunger for great barbecue. For more than 17 years, they have been serving oak-smoked barbecue cooked low and slow in the Texas tradition—no shortcuts, just smoke and time. Some can cook it faster, but no one cooks it better than Bunkhouse. Everyone loves their tender brisket, sweet glazed ribs, perfectly seasoned sausage, encrusted pork loin, ham, turkey, pulled pork, and all the fix'ins. Stop by. You'll be glad you did.

**Tuesday – Saturday: 11:00 am to 8:00 pm**

## All-Purpose Seasoning

¼ cup salt

¼ cup sugar

⅛ cup paprika

⅛ cup garlic powder

1 tablespoon turmeric

1 tablespoon cumin

1 tablespoon course black pepper

Mix all ingredients well and store in an airtight container. Good on all types of meat—brisket, ribs, chicken, and more.

**Restaurant Recipe**

## Bunkhouse Barbeque Sauce

16 ounces good tomato sauce

½ cup water

¼ cup vinegar

2 tablespoons brown sugar

2 tablespoons onion powder

2 tablespoons Worcestershire sauce

2 tablespoons coarse black pepper

1 tablespoon garlic powder

1 tablespoon paprika

Combine all ingredients in a heavy saucepan and simmer until desired thickness, about 30 minutes. If it gets too thick, add a small amount of water.

**Restaurant Recipe**

## Rick's Cheesecake

*Filling:*

3 pounds cream cheese, softened

1½ cups sugar

⅔ cup sour cream

3 eggs

3 tablespoons pure vanilla extract

2 tablespoons lemon juice

In a mixer, cream the cream cheese. Add sugar and mix until well blended. Add sour cream; mix well. Add eggs, one at a time, mixing well after each, until blended. Add vanilla slowly while mixing on low speed. Add lemon juice; mix until smooth.

*Crust:*

2 cups graham cracker crumbs

½ cup sugar

⅔ cup butter, melted

Line the bottom of a 10-inch springform pan with parchment paper. Combine crust ingredients and press into bottom and sides. Pour in filling, smooth out the top and bake at 250° for 1 hour and 25 minutes. Turn oven off and cool in oven another 1 hour and 25 minutes. Continue to cool at room temperature. Place in freezer until firm. Remove from pan, place on a cake board and cut in 14 to 16 slices. Serve plain or with toppings. Enjoy.

**Restaurant Recipe**

# AwShucks Oyster Bar

**3601 Greenville Avenue**
**Dallas, TX 75206**
**214-821-9449**
**www.awshucksdallas.com**

**OTHER LOCATIONS:**
AwShucks Oyster Bar
1630 South Stemmons
Freeway
Lewisville, TX 75067
972-436-2520

AwShucks Oyster Bar
4710 Preston Road
Frisco, TX 75034
972-294-5218

AwShucks Oyster Bar
6509 West Park Boulevard
Plano, TX 75093
214-440-2570

Big Shucks Oyster Bar
103 South Coit Road
Richardson, TX 75080
972-231-8202

Big Shucks Oyster Bar
6232 East Mockingbird Lane
Dallas, TX 75214
214-887-6353

In 1983, AwShucks Oyster Bar opened in a run-down former juice stand on Dallas' historic Greenville Avenue. With a commitment to the highest quality seafood, and a fun beach-like atmosphere, AwShucks has grown to six locations and become a true Dallas landmark. For more than 30 years, AwShucks has been dishing out fried baskets of Mississippi catfish, gulf shrimp, fresh gulf oysters, trays of boiled crab legs, shrimp, crawfish, and homemade sides. All customers pay on the honor system. When you are ready to leave, simply walk up to the cashier and tell them what you had. Swimsuits to tuxedos, everyone is welcome.

**Sunday – Thursday: 11:00 am to 10:00 pm**
**Friday & Saturday: 11:00 am to 11:00 pm**

## Beer Battered Fish Tacos

### Spicy Coleslaw:

1 pound green cabbage, finely diced

¾ cup diced tomatoes

¼ cup chopped cilantro

¾ cup lemon juice

¼ cup Louisiana-style hot sauce

2 tablespoons Worcestershire sauce

½ tablespoon black pepper

½ tablespoon salt

Mix all ingredients together.

### Tacos:

Soy oil for frying

2½ cups all-purpose flour

2 to 2¼ cups Dos Equis Special Lager

½ tablespoon garlic powder

½ tablespoon cayenne pepper

1 tablespoon Worcestershire sauce

6 (3- to 5-ounce) catfish fillets, cut in half length wise (or other white fish)

12 corn tortillas

4 cups prepared rice

1 avocado, sliced

1 cup ranch dressing

Heat oil to 350°. In a bowl, whisk flour, lager, garlic, pepper and Worcestershire together until smooth and lump free. Dip fillets in batter; let excess drip off. Carefully fry in oil till golden brown (about 5 minutes). Roll cooked fish in tortillas; serve with rice, spicy coleslaw, avocado slices, and ranch dressing.

**Restaurant Recipe**

## Cassie's Homemade Key Lime Pie

### Crust:

2 cups graham crackers

½ cup sugar

¼ pound margarine, softened

Mix all ingredients until crumbly. Press evenly on bottom and side of 8½-inch springform pan. Bake on a sheet pan at 350° for 25 minutes.

### Filling:

2 (14-ounce) cans sweetened condensed milk

8 egg yolks

¼ cup fresh Key lime juice

Whisk together all filling ingredients until smooth; pour into crust. Bake 25 to 30 minutes. Let cool 30 to 45 minutes. Refrigerate till ready to serve.

### Topping:

2 cups heavy cream

½ cup sugar

1 teaspoon pure vanilla extract

Beat all topping ingredients until stiff peaks form. Spread on top of pie; smooth till level. Release pan, cut and serve.

**Restaurant Recipe**

# Garden Café

**5310 Junius Street**
**Dallas, TX 75214**
**214-887-8330**

Garden Café is a daytime neighborhood eatery with an herb & vegetable garden around the patio. One of the most unique restaurants in Dallas, they feature southern-style breakfast and lunch. Some of the ingredients are sourced from their own organic garden surrounding the beautiful patio, and much of the rest comes from local farms. Serving organic pasture-raised eggs, direct source coffee, whole animal butchered meats, and local produce, you would be hard-pressed to find any restaurant with as much made-from-scratch fresh food. Join them for a Poetry Dinner event with a three-course meal followed by open mic poetry. They also feature local rotating art, artist receptions, book signings, and local musicians.

**7 days a week: 7:00 am to 3:00 pm**

## Acorn Squash Cake with Bourbon Whip Cream

**6½ cups all-purpose flour**

**1½ teaspoons baking soda**

**1½ teaspoons baking powder**

**¼ teaspoon salt**

**½ teaspoon nutmeg**

**2 tablespoons cinnamon**

**3½ cups baked squash (acorn or butternut squash are best)**

**3 cups Texas Honeybee Guild Honey or maple syrup**

**¾ pound butter, very soft**

**6 eggs**

In a bowl, whisk flour, baking soda, baking powder, salt, nutmeg and cinnamon: set aside. In another bowl, whisk squash, honey or syrup, butter and eggs; set aside. Add flour mixture to squash mixture; fold until combined. Pour into greased 10x12-inch pan. Bake 30 minutes at 350°.

### Bourbon Whip Cream:

**1 cup heavy cream**

**2 tablespoons sugar**

**1 teaspoon cinnamon**

**2 tablespoons top shelf bourbon**

Whip cream with sugar and cinnamon until thick. Add bourbon: whisk to combine. Spoon on cut slices of cake before serving.

**Family Favorite**

## Flat Iron Steak & Eggs with Homestead Gristmill Herbed Grits

### Grits:

**8 cups chicken stock**

**1 cup organic yellow grits**

**½ cup heavy cream**

**2 tablespoons butter**

**2 teaspoons salt**

**2 teaspoons pepper**

**1 teaspoon cayenne powder**

**2 tablespoons thyme**

**1 tablespoon rosemary**

In saucepan, bring chicken stock to a boil; whisk in grits. Turn heat to medium; cook 40 minutes, whisking often. Add cream, butter, salt, pepper, cayenne, thyme and rosemary. Set aside; keep warm.

### Steak & Eggs:

**4 flat iron steaks**

**Coarse-ground kosher salt**

**Coarse-ground black peppercorn**

**2 eggs, cooked over easy**

Season steaks with salt and pepper; let rest 15 minutes at room temperature. Heat cast-iron pan over high heat; sear each side of steak 2 minutes. Finish in 350° oven until done to taste. Plate grits, steak and end with eggs on top.

**Restaurant Recipe**

# Hypnotic Donuts & Biscuits

*Road trip worthy. Road trip approved. When you are here, everything is better.*

www.hypnoticdonuts.com • Facebook, Twitter, and Instagram: hypnoticdonuts

**DALLAS LOCATION:**
**9007 Garland Road**
**Dallas, TX 75218**
**214-668-6999**

Monday – Friday: 6:30 am to 12:00 pm
Saturday: 7:30 am to 1:00 pm
Sunday: 8:00 am to 2:00 pm

**DENTON LOCATION:**
**235 West Hickory Street**
**Denton, TX 76201**
**940-390-1486**

Monday – Friday: 7:30 am to 2:00 pm
Saturday & Sunday: 8:00 am to 3:00 pm

Hypnotic Donuts & Biscuits is ranked as one of the top donut shops in America by several publications so you are guaranteed to love their unique and delicious donuts. Do not forget to try one of their award-winning chicken biscuits; they are not like any chicken biscuits you have had before. They take donuts and chicken biscuits to the next level of taste.

## Good Times Queso

*We call this family favorite "Good Times Queso," because every time it is served we are having good times—during the holidays or while watching sports or movies with family and friends. Occasionally at our store we offer a biscuit of the month that has Good Times Queso on it.*

**1 (1-pound) package hot (spicy) breakfast sausage**

**1 jalapeño, diced**

**1 onion, diced**

**1 (2-pound) block Velveeta cheese**

**1 (10-ounce) can diced tomatoes with green chiles (Rotel)**

**2 (4-ounce) cans chopped green chiles**

**3 avocados**

**1 lime**

**1 (8-ounce) carton sour cream**

**Chips, for dipping (recommend Tostitos Hint of Lime)**

Brown sausage, jalapeño and onion in a large nonstick skillet; drain. Reduce heat to low. Chop Velveeta into cubes and add to sausage mixture. Add tomatoes and green chiles (with juice for both). Cook, stirring frequently, until cheese is completely melted. While cooking, peel avocados and remove pit. Put into a bowl and smash up; squeeze in lime juice and mix. Pour queso into a large serving bowl. Top one side with avocado and one side with sour cream. (Optional, serve in small bowls and have avocado and sour cream sitting next to it for people to add as they wish.) Serve with chips.

**Family Favorite**

## The Hulk

*This is a base mix for a great protein shake. With this base you can let your taste buds and imagination run free. Add your choice of ingredients and quantity to taste. We've included some of our favorite combinations.*

*Base:*

**½ cup water**

**8 or 9 ice cubes**

**1 scoop plain or vanilla protein powder**

**½ cup nonfat Greek yogurt**

**½ cup nonfat cottage cheese**

In blender, add water, then ice. Add remaining ingredients in any order. Blend on low to crush ice. Switch to high and blend until smooth.

*Some of our favorite add-ins:*

*Wake Up:*

**Substitute chocolate protein powder (instead of plain)**

**1 tablespoon Ovaltine**

**2 tablespoons instant coffee**

*Yellow Berry:*

**½ banana, chopped**

**1 handful strawberries**

*Nutty Nanner:*

**Substitute chocolate protein (instead of plain)**

**½ tablespoon P2B peanut butter powder**

**½ banana, chopped**

**Restaurant Recipe**

JUST GOOD FOOD

# HAMBURGERS

## ROAST BEEF SANDWICHES

## John's Café

**1733 Greenville Avenue**
**Dallas, TX 75206**
**214-874-0800 • www.johns-cafe.com**

John's Café is a true family business run by daughter, Georgia, her mom, Mary, and dad, John Spiros, who came to the United States from Greece in 1970 with his huge Greek family. The eldest of seven, John worked very hard at odd jobs to help support his family. His dream began in 1972 when he opened John's Café, which is now a Dallas institution serving many generations of families through the years. As people walk in the door, John greets them from behind the counter. Food is made to order and served hot and fresh. John's is a family-style place where you feel at home; that's why they've been around for more than 40 years.

**Monday – Saturday: 7:00 am to 3:00 pm**
**Sunday: 8:00 am to 2:00 pm**

## John's Greek Salad with Pita Bread

*This is a wonderful, light and fresh salad that is great year-round.*

**1 medium head iceberg lettuce, chopped**

**1 medium cucumber, sliced**

**1 to 2 small tomatoes, cut into wedges**

**Kalamata olives, drained and sliced**

**1 white or red onion, chopped**

**8 ounces crumbled feta cheese**

**Pepperoncini peppers**

Combine all ingredients in a large salad bowl and toss to combine.

### Dressing:

**¼ cup olive oil**

**3 tablespoons red wine vinegar**

**1 teaspoon dried oregano**

**½ teaspoon salt**

**⅛ teaspoon pepper**

In a small bowl, whisk together all dressing ingredients. Drizzle over salad and toss to coat. Serve with pita bread on the side or top will grilled chicken to make a meal.

**Restaurant Recipe**

## Gyro Omelet

*This is one of our top-selling omelets all these years. It's really delicious if you want to venture out and try something different.*

**½ cup chopped onion**

**½ cup chopped tomato**

**½ cup chopped bell pepper**

**3 eggs**

**4 to 5 thin slices precooked gyro meat**

**4 tablespoons feta cheese or Swiss cheese**

Grill veggies until hot. Beat eggs, obviously, for omelet. Pour in skillet (or on grill) and cook evenly. Top with meat, veggies and cheese. Fold and allow omelet to finish, remove from heat and enjoy.

**Restaurant Recipe**

# JR's Barn

### 1430 North Temple Drive
### Diboll, TX 75941
### 936-829-4141

JR's Barn is a one-stop shop that looks forward to taking care of all your needs. The tearoom and coffee shop will serve you a lite lunch of sandwiches, soups, and baked potatoes or sweets like cupcakes, pies, and more. You can dine-in or order out. Catering is also available. Check out Vintage Blooms where they will take care of all your floral needs. Don't forget to visit the gift shop to pick out your special gifts.

**Monday – Friday: 9:00 am to 5:00 pm**

## Broccoli Cornbread

1 (8.5-ounce) box Jiffy cornbread mix

4 eggs

1 (16-ounce) package frozen broccoli, thawed, chopped and drained

1 stick butter, melted

1 onion, chopped

1 (8-ounce) carton sour cream

Jalapeño or red pepper to taste

Mix all ingredients together. Spray a 9x13-inch pan; pour in batter. Bake at 350° until done.

**Restaurant Recipe**

## Chocolate Chip Cookies

1 cup butter-flavored Crisco

¾ cup brown sugar

¾ cup sugar

2 eggs

1 teaspoon vanilla

2¼ cups all-purpose flour

1 teaspoon baking soda

1 teaspoon salt

1 bag semisweet chocolate chips

Preheat oven to 375°. Cream shortening and sugars; add eggs and vanilla. Add dry ingredients; mix until combined. Fold in chocolate chips. Roll dough into 1-inch balls; place on a cookie sheets. Bake 10 minutes. Makes 30 to 40 cookies.

**Family Favorite**

## Crawfish Soup

½ onion, chopped

1 stick butter

1 (10-ounce) can Rotel tomatoes

1 (15-ounce) can whole-kernel corn

2 (10.75-ounce) cans cream of potato soup

1 pint half-and- half

1 pound crawfish tails

Tony Chachere's Creole seasoning to taste

Sauté onion in butter. Add remaining ingredients, except crawfish; heat through. Add crawfish; cook 30 minutes.

**Restaurant Recipe**

## Pralines

1 (16-ounce) box light brown sugar

1 cup whipping cream

3 cups chopped or halved pecans

2 tablespoons butter

In a microwave bowl, combine sugar with whipping cream; mix well. Microwave 11 to 12 minutes. Remove from microwave; add butter and pecans. Stir until starts to thicken; drop by spoonfuls onto wax paper.

**Restaurant Recipe**

# Vincek's Smokehouse

**139 South Dill Street**
**East Bernard, TX 77435**
**979-335-7921**
**www.vincekssmokehouseinc.com**
**Find us on Facebook**

Charles Ray "C.R." Vincek and wife Lois, along with their son Gary, and daughter Cheryl Failla, started their family business in 1985 at their present location on Highway 60. Quality and Vincek's pecan wood smoked meats and treats have earned Vincek's Smokehouse many repeat customers in their 30 years of business. The smokehouse features a full-service meat market with the freshest cuts of meat, such as pecan-smoked sausage, beef sticks, jerky, and summer sausage. Barbecue and lunch specials are served daily, and the bakery case features tasty homemade meat and fruit kolaches, cookies, cakes, and individual pies.

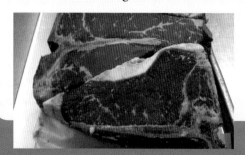

**Tuesday – Saturday: 7:00 am to 6:00 pm**
**Sunday: 8:00 am to 3:00 pm**

## Chicken Spaghetti

1 fryer

3 ribs celery, chopped

2 onions, chopped

2 cloves garlic, chopped

1 (4-ounce) can sliced mushrooms, drained

1 (12-ounce) package spaghetti

1 (15-ounce) can chopped tomatoes

2 tablespoons chopped black olives

1 (10.75-ounce) can cream of mushroom soup

Salt and pepper to taste

Few dashes Worcestershire sauce

1 pound Velveeta cheese, grated

Simmer chicken in well-seasoned water. Remove chicken from broth. Let cool; debone. Measure 1 quart broth; pour into a stockpot. Add celery, onions, garlic and mushrooms; cook for a few minutes. Add spaghetti; cook 7 to 8 minutes, stirring occasionally. Add tomatoes, olives, soup, salt and pepper. Add Worcestershire sauce and cheese to boned chicken; mix into the spaghetti mixture. Pour into a large Pyrex dish. Bake covered at 350° for approximately 35 minutes.

**Restaurant Recipe**

## Texas Sheet Cake

1 cup water

3 tablespoons cocoa

1 cup margarine

2 cups sugar

2 cups all-purpose flour

1 teaspoon baking soda

1 teaspoon cinnamon

½ cup buttermilk

2 eggs

1 teaspoon vanilla

Combine water, cocoa and margarine in a saucepan; bring to a light boil. Combine dry ingredients in large mixing bowl. Add hot mixture; mix well. Stir in remaining ingredients. Pour into greased 14x18-inch pan. Bake at 350° for 20 to 30 minutes or until done. Make icing while cake is baking.

### Icing:

½ cup margarine

3 tablespoons cocoa

⅓ cup milk

1 pound powdered sugar

1 teaspoon vanilla

1 cup chopped pecans

Melt margarine, cocoa and milk in a saucepan over medium heat. Remove from heat and stir in powdered sugar, vanilla and pecans. Spread over hot cake.

**Restaurant Recipe**

# Sam's Original Restaurant

**390 East I-45**
**Fairfield, TX 75840**
**903-389-7267**

**www.samsrestaurant.com**

Sam's Restaurant is a third-generation family-owned business that has been serving up delicious barbecue and homemade country dishes for more than 60 years. They are most famous for the daily-baked homemade pies with "mile high" meringue, Texas-style barbecue and all you can eat buffet. If you leave hungry, it's your fault.

**7 days a week: 6:00 am to 10:00 pm**

## Sam's Original Homemade Bread

1 cup Crisco

1 cup Kellogg's All-Bran

1 cup boiling water

2 (.25-ounce) packages instant dry yeast

1 cup warm water

2 eggs, beaten

¾ cup sugar

1 teaspoon salt

6 cups all-purpose flour

Combine Crisco, All-Bran and boiling water. Mix and set aside. Dissolve yeast in warm water; add eggs, sugar, and salt. Stir in All-Bran mixture. Add flour and knead. Let rise 1 hour. Knead; put into 1 large or 2 small treated loaf pans. Let rise again 1 hour. Bake approximately 45 minutes at 300° or until done.

**Restaurant Recipe**

## Small Bread Pudding

10 homemade biscuits (1 to 2 days old is preferred)

½ gallon milk

3 cups sugar

4 eggs

¼ teaspoon cinnamon

2 tablespoons vanilla

Yellow food coloring (optional)

Combine all ingredients and place in a greased casserole dish. Bake at 350° approximately 45 minutes or until lightly browned and toothpick comes out clean.

*Vanilla Sauce:*

1 quart milk

½ cup sugar

1 teaspoon vanilla

1 teaspoon cornstarch

Raisins to taste

Yellow food coloring (optional)

Combine all ingredients in a double boiler. Bring to a simmer, stirring constantly. Cook until desired thickness is reached. Cool slightly and pour over top of bread pudding.

**Restaurant Recipe**

# JuJu's Cajun Crawfish Shak

**18277 Highway 365 • Fannett, TX 77705**
**409-794-2020**
**Find us on Facebook**

JuJu's Cajun Crawfish Shak sits alongside a lonely stretch of Farm Market 365 in Fannett. Lacy Carter and her father, Don Hanks, opened Juju's in 2003, serving up the most delicious crawfish in all of southeast Texas—some would claim the world. Open only during crawfish season, JuJu's keeps the menu simple, serving only crawfish by the pound, corn, and potatoes. They also offer canned sodas and bottled water, but guests are welcome to BYOB. Come and let JuJu's cook you up a batch of crawdads, and join the family like so many others have. You'll be glad you did.

**Tuesday – Saturday:**
**11:00 am to 8:00 pm**
**Sunday:**
**11:00 am to 6:00 pm**

## Crab Cakes or Deviled Crab

½ cup chopped white onion

¼ cup diced celery

3 tablespoons butter

¾ cup crushed crackers or dry bread crumbs, plus additional for dusting

½ teaspoon dry mustard

½ teaspoon paprika

1 teaspoon Worcestershire sauce

¼ cup chopped parsley

Tabasco sauce to taste

Salt and pepper to taste

½ cup milk or cream

2 eggs, beaten

1 pound crabmeat

Sauté onion and celery in butter till translucent. Add crumbs and seasonings. Mix in milk, eggs and crabmeat. Shape into cakes; dust with additional crumbs. Brown in cooking oil or butter; serve hot.

For Deviled Crab: Mix as above. But put the filling into crab shells or sea shells and dust with bread crumbs; bake 15 minutes at 350°. Mix can also be used for stuffing fish, lobster, shrimp or game birds.

**Restaurant Recipe**

# Star Drug Store

**510 23rd Street**
**Galveston, TX 77550**
**409-766-7719**
**www.galvestonstardrug.com**

In 1886, renowned architect Nicholas Clayton designed the building now known as the Star Drug Store in Galveston, Texas. The building was renovated in 1905 to house what is considered today as the "Oldest Drug Store in Texas, circa 1890's." The building functioned as a drug store into the mid 1980's where it continued on as a lunch counter and soda fountain. After a fire in 1998, the Tilts family purchased the building at the end of 2001, and spent the next 5 years lovingly renovating and restoring the façade, the historical Coca-Cola neon porcelain sign, and the drug store itself. Patrons now can still sit at the original horseshoe counter built in 1915—complete with embedded red star in its prominent face—that still reigns as Star Drug Store's most recognized emblem. Serving breakfast and lunch, the Star Drug Store's nostalgic menu offers juicy burgers, classic sandwiches, daily specials, refreshing fountain drinks, and sweet treats that have been served for generations.

**7 days a week:**
**8:30 am to 3:00 pm**

## Island Pork Press Sandwich Special

10 pounds boneless pork loin

Teriyaki sauce to taste

Orange juice to cover

Juice of 1 lime

Sliced onion

Sliced pineapple

Raspberry chipotle sauce

Butter, softened

Baguette, thick sliced

Marinate pork loin in a teriyaki, orange juice and lime citrus marinade overnight. Roast in 350° oven for 45 minutes or until fully cooked. Slice into half-inch-thick slices. Sauté onion and pineapple in raspberry chipotle sauce until caramelized. Butter baguette and place butter-side-down on grill. Layer pork, caramelized onions and pineapple slice onto bread. Top with another slice of bread. Place either a brick wrapped in aluminum foil or a press on to the sandwich, grill each side until edges are brown. Serve with extra raspberry chipotle sauce for dipping, if desired.

**Restaurant Recipe**

## Shipwreck Float

1 tablespoon cherry syrup

Splash Dr. Pepper, Coke and Root Beer

Vanilla ice cream

Cookies or brownies, whipped cream and a cherry, garnish

Mix cherry syrup and sodas in a tall fountain glass, filling it a little over halfway. Add 2 scoops vanilla ice cream. Garnish with cookies or brownies, whip cream and cherry on top.

**Restaurant Recipe**

## "Dill-icious" Potato Salad

1 pound red potatoes, cut into small chunks and cooked

½ cup sour cream or more

½ cup mayonnaise or more

¾ to 1 small onion, finely chopped

25 to 30 pimento-stuffed green olives, finely chopped (and a little olive juice)

Dill seasoning

Salt and pepper to taste

Place cooked potatoes in a large bowl. Combine sour cream and mayonnaise until creamy. Add to potatoes with onion, olives and seasoning to taste; mix. Add a little olive juice; mix. Taste and add more olives or onion to taste.

**Restaurant Recipe**

## Hello, Sweetie!

**2200 South Austin Avenue, Suite 101**
**Georgetown, TX 78626**
**512-869-3304**
**www.facebook.com/HelloSweetieBBQ**

Hello, Sweetie! captures the flavor of Texas with pit-smoked barbecue, and features a delicious relish made from sweet peppers as well as yummy desserts, including Blue Bell ice cream. Located in Georgetown, Texas, this cozy barbecue joint evokes the traditions of the region with a tasty twist. Everyone is greeted with a "Hello, Sweetie!" and the aroma of brisket on the pit is a sure-fire invitation to a delicious meal. Along with the pulled pork, the distinctive flavors found in the beans, coleslaw, and potato salad are local favorites. Catering is available.

**Monday – Saturday: 11:00 am to 8:00 pm**

Hello Sweetie!

# Riverhouse Grill

## RESTAURANT & SPECIAL EVENTS

**210 Southwest Barnard Street**
**Glen Rose, TX 76043**
**254-898-8514**
**www.theriverhousegrill.net**

This family-owned restaurant offers small-town hospitality within a renovated historic home located one block from the quaint downtown area of Glen Rose. Chef and owner, Milan Olejnik Jr., puts thought and detail into each dish he prepares, serving only the freshest meats and vegetables with house-made sauces and desserts. The restaurant's setting, within a stunning home built in 1903, offers a dining experience like no other. Whether a casual lunch on the patio, brunch in the main dining downstairs, or fine dining in a private room upstairs, they cover it all. As they say, "Whatever the occasion, our Riverhouse is your Riverhouse."

**Wednesday – Saturday: Lunch 11:00 am to 2:00 pm; Dinner 5:00 pm to 9:00 pm**
**Sunday: Brunch 11:00 am to 2:00 pm**

*Monday and Tuesday are reserved by reservation for parties of 20 or more.*

## Lobster Bisque

1 pound butter
1 large yellow onion, finely chopped
1 bunch celery, finely chopped
2 cups all-purpose flour
6 bay leaves
4 ounces lobster base
½ cup paprika
2 quarts water
1 quart heavy cream
1 tablespoon white pepper
1 cup bourbon

Sauté onion and celery in butter in a large saucepan. Mix in flour; cook 2 minutes, stirring constantly. Add bay leaves, lobster base, paprika and water; bring to a boil. Remove bay leaves; whisk until smooth and thick. Add cream, white pepper and bourbon; mix well. Hat through, but do not allow to boil after adding cream.

**Restaurant Recipe**

## White Chocolate & Cranberry Bread Pudding with White Chocolate Vanilla Bourbon Sauce

6 cups milk

6 cups sugar

15 eggs

1 tablespoon vanilla

6 cups stale bread, cubed

2 cups dried cranberries

2 cups white chocolate chips

Preheat oven to 350°. Grease large baking pan. Combine milk, sugar, eggs and vanilla in mixing bowl. Place cubed bread into greased pan; pour egg mixture over top. Sprinkle with cranberries and white chocolate chips; fold into mixture. Let sit about 10 minutes until bread has soaked up almost half of mixture.

### Topping:

1 cup butter, softened

1 cup sugar

1 cup brown sugar

1 cup all-purpose flour

1 tablespoon cinnamon

¼ teaspoon nutmeg

1 cup chopped pecans or walnuts

Cream butter and sugars together. Mix in flour, cinnamon, nutmeg and nuts. Crumble topping evenly over bread pudding. Bake at 350° for 1 to 1½ hours until a toothpick comes out clean.

### White Chocolate Vanilla Bourbon Sauce:

2 cups white chocolate chips

2 cups heavy cream

2 tablespoons bourbon

1 teaspoon vanilla extract

Put white chocolate chips in a bowl. Heat heavy cream in a saucepan until hot. Pour over chips and whisk until combined. Add bourbon and vanilla; mix well. Drizzle over bread pudding when serving.

**Restaurant Recipe**

## MOTHER'S KITCHEN

**3962 State Highway 43 East**
**Henderson, TX 75652**
**903-836-4440**
**www.facebook.com/**
**MothersKitchen.Henderson**

Family owned and operated, Mother's Kitchen is located 3.8 miles outside of Henderson's city limits. This outstanding restaurant was established in 2011 when owner and head chef Mary Jackson Ferdowsijah's passion for cooking  influenced her to retire from her nursing career to become a small business owner. Mother's is a home-style cooking restaurant serving daily specials, desserts, and every day menu items like chicken & dressing, meatloaf, hot water cornbread, and buttermilk pie, all prepared daily from fresh ingredients. They are sharing a few of their recipes in hopes of convincing readers that delicious, homemade meals aren't as hard as they seem.

**Monday – Friday: 9:30 am to 4:00 pm**
**Saturday: 9:30 am to 2:00 pm**

## Southern-Style Collard Greens

**2 to 3 pounds collard greens**
**8 thick slices hog jowl or bacon**
**8 cups water**
**1½ cups chopped yellow onions**
**1 tablespoon salt**
**½ tablespoon pepper**
**Crushed red pepper (optional)**
**Dash seasoned salt**
**1 tablespoon apple cider vinegar**
**1 tablespoon extra virgin olive oil**

Place collards in sink or bowl; wash thoroughly using about 3 water changes. Continue washing until no sediment can be felt in bottom of the sink or bowl. Remove stems from collard leafs by grasping stem with one hand and pulling leaf away with the other hand. Also remove any thick veins. Roll leaves and cut into ½-inch strips, or chop coarsely. Cook jowl or bacon in a skillet, reserving drippings for collards or for another recipe. Bring a pot of water to a boil; add onion, cooked jowl, salt, pepper, crushed red pepper and seasoned salt. Add greens, vinegar, olive oil and pan drippings, if desired. Cover; simmer over medium to low heat for about 1 hour or until greens are tender. May serve with meatloaf, purple hull peas and hot water cornbread. Makes 6 to 8 servings.

**Restaurant Recipe**

## Chicken Spaghetti

**3 boneless skinless chicken breasts**
**1 (8-ounce) package spaghetti**
**1 pound Velveeta cheese, diced**
**2 medium tomatoes, diced**
**1 green chile pepper, diced small**
**1 (10.75-ounce) can condensed
cream of chicken soup**
**1 pinch garlic powder**
**Salt and pepper to taste**

Boil chicken in a large pot with water to cover and salt to taste until done, about 30 minutes. Remove chicken from pot and set aside to cool; shred. Keep broth boiling. Put spaghetti in boiling broth and cook until al dente, 8 to 10 minutes; drain, discarding broth. Return spaghetti to pot; add cheese, tomatoes, chile pepper and soup. Cook over low heat, stirring constantly to prevent sticking, until melted and heated through. Season with garlic powder, salt and pepper to taste. (Optional, pour into a small baking dish and bake at 350° until bubbly.) Serve with a garden salad and garlic bread. Makes 9 servings.

**Restaurant Recipe**

## Coca-Cola Cake

**1 cup butter, softened**
**1¾ cups sugar**
**2 large eggs**
**2 teaspoons vanilla extract**
**2 cups all-purpose flour**
**¼ cup cocoa**
**1 teaspoon baking soda**
**1½ cups miniature marshmallows**
**½ cup buttermilk**
**1 cup Coca-Cola**
**¾ cup chopped pecans, toasted
(optional)**

Preheat oven to 350°. Beat butter on low speed with electric mixer until creamy. Gradually beat in sugar until blended. Add eggs and vanilla extract; beat at low speed until blended. Set aside. Combine flour, cocoa and baking soda. Gradually add to butter mixture. Beat at a low speed until blended. Stir in marshmallows, and pour batter into a greased and floured 9x13-inch pan. Bake 30 to 35 minutes or until fork comes out clean. Remove from oven and cool for 10 minutes. While cake is cooling, prepare frosting by mixing Coca-Cola and buttermilk. Add toasted chopped pecans, if desired. (Do not make frosting ahead.) Once the cake has cooled 10 minutes, pour Coca-Cola frosting over warm cake. Nothing like dessert to complete your meal.

**Restaurant Recipe**

# Barbecue Inn

**116 West Crosstimbers Street**
**Houston, TX 77018**
**713-695-8112**
**www.thebarbecueinn.com**
**Like us on Facebook**

Louis, Jr. and Wayne—"The Brothers"—learned the family business from an early age busing tables at The Barbecue Inn, which was founded in 1946 by their parents, Louis and Nell Skrehot. Their 50-year partnership, coupled with hard work, determination, and an entrepreneurial spirit are responsible for making the Barbecue Inn the thriving business

it is today. Local favorites include barbecue ribs that are "To-Die-For" plus the best fried seafood in the Gulf Coast area. The most popular menu item is the fried chicken, nationally recognized by *Travel & Leisure, Food & Wine,* and a host of others who agree it is some of the best fried chicken in the U.S.A.

**Tuesday – Saturday:**
**10:30 am to 9:30 pm**

## Spinach Dip

**2 cups Hellmann's Real mayonnaise**

**½ cup parsley sprigs**

**½ small onion, chopped**

**1 small garlic clove, minced**

**1 tablespoon lemon juice**

**¼ teaspoon pepper**

**1 (10-ounce) package frozen chopped spinach, thawed, drained well**

Blend all ingredients on high speed until finely chopped. Cover and refrigerate at least 4 hours or up to 2 days before serving. Makes 2 (¾-cup) servings.

**Family Favorite**

## Hot Crabmeat Hors D'oeuvre

**1 tablespoon melted butter**

**1 tablespoon flour**

**½ cup milk**

**1 tablespoon Sauterne wine**

**½ teaspoon salt**

**1 cup flaked crabmeat**

**Bread rounds**

**Parmesan cheese**

Cook butter, flour and milk over low heat until thick. Add wine, salt and crabmeat. Mix well; refrigerate. Just before serving, spread on bread, sprinkle with Parmesan and broil just until cheese is melted.

**Family Favorite**

## 22 Minute Cake

**2 cups sugar**

**2 cups all-purpose flour**

**1 cup water**

**1 stick real butter**

**½ cup vegetable oil**

**3½ teaspoons cocoa**

**½ cup buttermilk**

**2 eggs, beaten**

**1 teaspoon baking soda**

**1 teaspoon vanilla**

Do NOT use a mixer. Combine sugar and flour in a large bowl. In a small stockpot, combine water, butter, oil and cocoa over medium-high heat; bring to a boil. Pour over flour mixture and combine. In a separate bowl, combine buttermilk, eggs, baking soda and vanilla. Add to batter and mix well. Pour into greased 9x13-inch baking dish; bake 20 minutes at 400°. When cake has baked 18 minutes, begin making icing.

### Icing:

**1 stick real butter**

**½ cup milk**

**3½ teaspoons cocoa**

**1 (16-ounce) package powdered sugar**

**1 cup chopped nuts**

Combine butter, cocoa and milk in saucepan over medium heat. Bring to a boil. Remove from heat; add powdered sugar and nuts. Pour over hot cake.

**Family Favorite**

# Rio Ranch Steakhouse

**9999 Westheimer Road**
**Houston, TX 77042**
**713-952-5000**
**www.rioranch.com**

Centered on a 30-foot limestone fireplace, Rio Ranch showcases "cowboy elegance," warm hospitality and fine comfort foods in an authentic atmosphere inspired by the ranch houses of early Texas. Dine on fresh mesquite-grilled steaks or seafood in an extraordinary setting with a small group or in a private dining room for 10 to 200 guests. Enjoy tranquil patio dining as the babbling water flows over the county rocks in the man-made creek. Good food, excellent service, and a relaxing atmosphere is what you can expect when dining at Rio Ranch. Let them cater your next event.

**Monday – Thursday:**
**6:00 am to 10:00 pm**
**Friday:**
**6:00 am to 11:00 pm**
**Saturday:**
**7:00 am to 11:00 pm**
**Sunday:**
**7:00 am to 10:00 pm**

## Ranch Style Shrimp Salsa

**1 pound (16/20 count) shrimp, boiled and chopped**

**1 avocado, chopped**

**2 cups Rio Ranch Tomato Salsa (recipe below)**

**1 lime wedge**

**1 sprig cilantro**

In a bowl, combine shrimp, avocado and salsa. Mix well. Serve with lime wedge and cilantro sprig.

### Rio Ranch Tomato Salsa:

**2 slices red bell pepper**

**2 slices yellow bell pepper**

**8 slices tomatillos**

**½ red onion, sliced**

**4 cured jalapeños**

**1 (12-ounce) can tomato juice**

**¼ cup white vinegar**

**¼ cup maple syrup**

**1 (14-ounce) bottle ketchup**

**1 cup chopped cilantro**

**4 cloves garlic, minced**

**2 tablespoons kosher salt**

Grill bell peppers, tomatillos, onion and jalapeños over open fire until charred. Set aside to cool; peel. Purée in blender. Put in a bowl and stir in remaining ingredients. Refrigerate for 1 hour before serving.

**Restaurant Recipe**

## Rio Ranch Chicken Wings

**2 tablespoons kosher salt**

**¼ cup Rio Ranch seasoning (available at Rio Ranch)**

**2 tablespoons ground black pepper**

**12 chicken wings (wings and drums only)**

**5 cups vegetable oil**

**3 cups Rio Ranch Spicy Black Sauce (available at Rio Ranch)**

Combine salt, Rio Ranch seasoning and black pepper in a bowl; toss with wings. In a deep fryer or shallow pan, heat oil to 375°. Add half the wings. Stirring occasionally, cook until wings reach internal temperature of 165°. Remove wings; set aside to cool down. After 5 minutes, while wings are still warm, toss in a bowl with Rio Ranch Black Sauce. Add remaining half of the wings into the fryer; repeat the process.

**Restaurant Recipe**

# McKenzie's Barbeque & Burgers

**1706 11th Street • Huntsville, TX 77320**
**936-291-7347**
**www.mckenziesbarbeque.com**

When it comes to great barbeque, the secret is preparation and planning. Real barbeque starts with the best cuts of meat, slow-cooked and smoked over hardwood for up to 22 hours in a rotating pit specifically designed by barbeque experts with decades of experience. Shortcuts do not make for great barbeque. Great barbeque taste comes from great cuts of meat. Add the sauce—and McKenzie's has a great one you can take home—once the barbeque is slow-cooked to perfection. For great barbeque, trust McKenzie's. You have McKenzie's word—and McKenzie's name—on it.

**Monday – Thursday: 10:30 am to 8:00 pm**
**Friday – Saturday: 10:30 am to 9:00 pm**

## Meal in a Milk Can

36 ears corn, snub the ends and
leave in shucks
1 (10-gallon) milk can with lid
(drill small hole in lid)
4 heads cabbage, quartered
5 pounds potatoes, washed
3 onions, quartered
15 pounds smoked sausage
1 gallon water
1 penny

Stand corn, end-side down, in bottom
of milk can, making first layer. Add
cabbage, potatoes, onions and sausage
in this order. Pour in water. Place lid on;
put penny over hole in lid. Place over
low flame on butane burner. Cook until
penny blows off hole, approximately 45
minutes. Your nose will let you know
that it's time to turn the fire out. Cool
10 to 20 minutes. Pour into cooler for
serving.

**Family Favorite**

## Honey-Roasted Pork

1 (2- to 3-pound) boneless pork loin
roast
¼ cup honey
2 tablespoons Dijon mustard
½ teaspoon dried thyme
2 tablespoons mixed or black
peppercorns
½ teaspoon salt

Place roast on greased rack in shallow
foil-lined pan. Combine remaining
ingredients; brush half of mixture over
roast. Bake at 325° for 1 hour. Brush
remaining half of mixture over roast;
bake 30 minutes more or until internal
temperature registers 155°. Tent foil over
roast; let rest 10 minutes before slicing.

**Katherine Smith McKenzie
Restaurant Recipe**

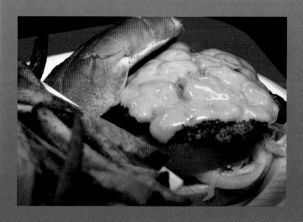

# Lone Star Grill

**13450 Highway 7 East**
**Joaquin, TX 75954**
**936-269-9665**

Lone Star Grill, a family owned and operated business with a country atmosphere, has a desire to make you feel at home. The burgers are six-ounce patties made with freshly ground beef and are never frozen. They hand-batter all fried foods and offer several specialty burgers and sandwiches. You will love it all, as everything is cooked to order to assure you the highest quality and freshness. At Lone Star Grill, you are greeted with a smile as they strive to give the greatest service experience so you will come back for more.

**Monday – Saturday: 7:00 am to 8:00 pm**

## Mexican Stack

4 pounds ground beef

5 large onions, chopped and divided

2 (14.5-ounce) cans chopped tomatoes

2 (15-ounce) cans tomato sauce

2 (12-ounce) cans tomato purée

1 teaspoon garlic powder

6 teaspoons salt

4 tablespoons chili powder

2 teaspoons cumin

2 (23-ounce) cans Ranch Style Beans

2 (12-ounce) bags corn chips

1 (14-ounce) bag rice, cooked

1 head lettuce, chopped

6 to 8 tomatoes, chopped

1 (14-ounce) can ripe olives

1 cup chopped pecans

1 (7-ounce) can flaked coconut

1 (16-ounce) jar picante sauce

1 pound shredded cheese

Brown beef with 3 chopped onions; drain. Add canned tomato products and seasonings; simmer 1 to 1½ hours. Add beans and heat through. In a large serving bowl, layer corn chips, rice, meat mixture, remaining 2 chopped onions, lettuce, tomatoes, olives, pecans, coconut, picante sauce and cheese. Serve.

**Family Favorite**

## Creamy Tacos

1½ pounds ground beef

1 large onion, chopped

1 to 2 (15-ounce) cans Ranch Style Beans

1 (10.75-ounce) can cream of mushroom soup

1 (10-ounce) can Rotel tomatoes

1 (5-ounce) can evaporated milk

1 pound Velveeta cheese, cubed

Brown ground beef with onions; drain. Add remaining ingredients. Heat until cheese is melted. Serve over rice or chips.

**Family Favorite**

## Smoked Sausage and Potatoes

3 to 5 potatoes, thinly sliced rounds

1 medium onion, thinly sliced and broken into rings

1 medium bell pepper, diced

2 (10-ounce) packages Mesquite or Polanski Kielbasa smoked sausage, thinly sliced

**Tex-Joy Mesquite Seasoning**

Using a 9x13-inch casserole dish, layer potatoes, onion, bell pepper and sausage in layers; sprinkle with seasoning. (Do not overspice.) Repeat layers until pan is full. Cook, covered with tin foil, at 350° until potatoes are tender.

**Family Favorite**

## RiverBend Restaurant

**211 Private Road 2422**
**Karnack, TX 75661**
**903-679-9000**
**www.facebook.com/RiverBend-Restaurant**

*Sunset from RiverBend deck*

The catfish are jumping, and alligators glide gracefully through the water as RiverBend customers enjoy beautiful views, savor delicious food, and experience the ambiance that is RiverBend Restaurant on Caddo Lake. The waterfront dining room offers views that change as often as the seasons. The large outdoor deck is ideal for those wishing to be near the natural wonders of Big Cypress River and Caddo Lake. The restaurant's specialty is golden fried catfish served with coleslaw, pinto beans, and jalapeño hushpuppies. The menu also offers steaks, shrimp, frog legs, crab cakes, and alligator, which are sure to please. Come by land or by water. Bring your friends and family to RiverBend.

**Wednesday & Thursday: 5:00 pm to 9:00 pm • Friday: 5:00 pm to 10:00 pm**
**Saturday: 11:00 am to 10:00 pm • Sunday: Noon to 7:00 pm**

## Chicken & Dumplings

*This is a family favorite from my grandmother, Pauline Loyd, or "Big Mama" as we all called her. My Aunt Quida Loyd Davis has mastered the taste and we all look forward to Christmas gatherings when she serves up a double batch of dumplings.*

**1 whole fryer or hen**

**Salt and pepper to taste**

**3 cups all-purpose flour**

**1 cup Crisco**

**2 eggs**

**Milk**

**1 (5-ounce) can evaporated milk**

Boil chicken in water to cover; season water with salt and pepper to taste. When done, remove chicken, reserving broth. Debone chicken, add meat back to broth and keep hot. In a bowl, combine flour and Crisco; cut together with fork and work like a pie crust. Add eggs, 1 teaspoon salt and enough milk to make a stiff dough. Do not overwork or it gets tough. Divide dough into 2 separate balls. Flour a large piece of wax paper and roll out dough very thin. Cut into 1x2-inch strips. Bring chicken and broth to a boil. (If broth isn't rich enough, add ½ stick butter.) Drop dumpling strips into broth 1 at a time so they do not stick together. Cook until dumplings are cooked through then add evaporated milk; season with pepper to taste. Cook 2 to 3 minutes more then remove from heat and leave covered about 40 to 45 minutes before serving.

**Family Favorite**

## Big Mama's Coconut Cake

*My mom, Janet Gibson Loyd, made this cake for my birthday every year. Always my favorite.*

**2 cups all-purpose flour**

**2 teaspoons baking powder**

**¼ teaspoon baking soda**

**1⅓ cups sugar**

**½ cup Crisco**

**2 eggs**

**1 cup buttermilk**

**2 teaspoons vanilla**

Sift dry ingredients together. In another bowl, cream sugar, Crisco and eggs. Add dry ingredients, alternating with buttermilk, mixing after each addition. Stir in vanilla. Line 2 (9-inch) cake pans with wax paper. Add batter and bake at 350° for 20 to 30 minutes. Cool in pans 5 minutes; remove to cool completely.

### *Icing:*

**1 cup sugar**

**2 tablespoons water**

**¼ cup Karo syrup (white)**

**3 egg whites**

**1 teaspoon vanilla**

**1 to 2 cups flaked coconut**

Mix sugar, water, syrup, and egg whites in double boiler over medium heat; bring to a boil. Beat 7 minutes with a hand mixer. Remove from heat; add vanilla. Frost bottom cake layer then sprinkle with coconut. Add 2nd layer; frost side and top of cake; sprinkle top with coconut. Best 2nd day, if stored covered.

**Family Favorite**

# Country Church Café

**307 West Main Street
Kennard, TX 75847
936-655-2292**

Country Church Café is a product of prayer: a prayer for purpose. Today this café continues to bring the community together in fellowship and great food. They are a simple business of great food, great company, and great service. The vision is bigger than just good food. It is their mission to make the customers feel welcomed and for them to leave happier than when they came in.

*"You shall love the Lord your God with all your heart, with all your soul, and with all your strength." —Deuteronomy 6:5*

**Monday – Friday: 7:00 am to 2:00 pm
THURSDAY NIGHT:
All you can eat Fried Catfish 5:00 pm to 8:00 pm
STEAK NIGHTS:
Friday: 5:30 pm to 9:00 pm
Saturday: 5:00 pm to 9:00 pm**

## Fried Green Tomatoes

2 cups milk

2 eggs, beaten

2 cups all-purpose flour

1½ teaspoons salt

1 teaspoon pepper

Tony Chachere's Creole seasoning to taste

2 green tomatoes, sliced medium thickness

In shallow bowl, mix milk and eggs; set aside. In another shallow bowl, whisk together flour, salt, pepper and Tony's seasoning. Dip tomato slices into milk mixture, then flour mixture 2 times each. Drop tomatoes into 335° fryer. Fry until golden brown. Serve with ranch dressing.

### Ranch Dressing:

2 quarts mayonnaise

½ gallon buttermilk

4 (1-ounce) packages dry ranch dressing mix

Whisk all together, refrigerate and serve.

**Restaurant Recipe**

## Peach Cobbler

2 boxes yellow cake mix

1 (29-ounce) can sliced peaches, drained

1½ cups packed brown sugar

2 sticks butter, melted

Coat 9x9-inch pan with cooking spray. Cover bottom of pan with 1 cup dry cake mix. Spread peaches evenly over top. Sprinkle brown sugar over peaches. Cover with remaining cake mix; pour butter over top. Bake at 350° for 35 to 45 minutes.

**Restaurant Recipe**

# Storm's Drive-in Restaurant

**201 North Key, Highway 281**
**Lampasas, TX 76550**
**512-556-6269**

**www.stormsrestaurants.com**

For more than 50 years, the Storm family has been feeding hungry travelers. Despite so many changes in the food industry during that time, Storm's continues to do things the way they did 50 years ago, like grinding their own beef to guarantee the flavor and quality of Storm's famous Texas hamburgers. Potatoes are sliced fresh every day for the best French fries around. From hamburgers to malts, fresh sandwiches to breakfast, or even a plate of fresh catfish and more, Storm's Drive-in Restaurant is the place to go.

**Sunday – Thursday: 7:00 am to 9:00 pm**
**Friday & Saturday: 7:00 am to 10:00 pm**

## Carmelitas

1 cup all-purpose flour

1 cup rolled oats

¾ cup brown sugar

½ teaspoon baking soda

¼ teaspoon salt

¾ cup butter, melted

1 (11-ounce) bag Caramel bits

5 tablespoons evaporated milk

6 ounces chocolate chips

¾ cup chopped pecans

Preheat oven to 350°. In mixing bowl, combine flour, oats, brown sugar, baking soda, salt and butter. Press half into greased 8x12-inch baking pan. Bake 10 minutes. While baking, heat caramel and milk until smooth and creamy. Remove from heat and set aside. After crust has baked 10 minutes, sprinkle chocolate chips and pecans on top. Cover with caramel mixture. Top with remaining oatmeal mixture. Bake an additional 15 minutes. Cool completely then refrigerate 2 hours before cutting into bars.

**Local Favorite**

## Black Beans & Yellow Rice

½ pound bacon, diced

1 medium onion, chopped

2 cloves garlic, crushed

2 cups uncooked rice

2½ teaspoons salt

¼ teaspoon ground turmeric

⅓ teaspoon crushed red pepper

4 cups water

½ green bell pepper, chopped

2 medium-size fresh tomatoes, chopped

½ cup chopped ham (fully cooked)

4 (16-ounce) cans black beans

Cook bacon in a heavy saucepan; drain. Add onion and garlic; cook until onion is translucent. Stir in rice, seasonings and water. Bring to a boil. Reduce heat, cover and simmer 10 minutes. Add bell pepper, tomatoes and ham; simmer 10 minutes longer or until rice is tender and liquid is absorbed. Heat beans until hot. Spoon yellow rice into serving bowls and top with black beans.

**Local Favorite**

# Leona Drug Store

**126 North Leona Boulevard**
**Leona, TX 75850**
**903-344-1105**
**www.leonadrugstore.com**

The Leona Drug Store was rebuilt in 1922 after a downtown fire destroyed the building. Restoration began in 2000, and it was reopened for business in 2001, with the original

look and layout from the 1920s. Leona Drug Store is connected to the Leona General Store next door by a working crank telephone. Gifts include candles, coffee, cookbooks, Texas history books, old crank telephones, cards, etc. Drinks are served from the soda fountain—no bottled drinks—using recipes from old drug store

publications. Just like the 1920s, Leona Drug Store serves shakes, malts, phosphates, floats, banana splits, hot fudge, limeades, and sodas.

**Thursday & Friday: 5:00 pm to 9:00 pm**
**Saturday: Noon to 9:00 pm**

## Old-Fashioned Cream Soda

**3 tablespoons half-and-half**

**3 tablespoons vanilla syrup**

**⅔ cup carbonated water**

**Ice**

Add half-and-half and vanilla syrup to a drinking cup. Add carbonated water and stir until foam reaches top of glass. Add ice and serve.

**Restaurant Recipe**

## Old-Fashioned Cherry Limeade

**3 tablespoons simple syrup**

**3 tablespoons maraschino cherry juice**

**½ lime, juiced**

**⅔ cup carbonated water**

**Ice**

Add simple syrup (2 parts water, 1 part sugar, cooked into a syrup), cherry juice and lime juice in a glass and stir. Add carbonated water; stir. Add ice.

**Restaurant Recipe**

## Leona Drug Store Hot Fudge Sauce

**1 cup butter**

**6 ounces bittersweet chocolate (Ghirardelli 60% Cacoa Premium Baking Chips)**

**1 cup sugar**

**1 cup brown sugar**

**1 cup cocoa**

**1 (12-ounce) can evaporated milk**

**1 teaspoon vanilla**

Melt butter and chocolate over low heat, continually stirring. Add sugar, brown sugar and cocoa. Stir until smooth. Add evaporated milk. Cook over medium heat, stirring constantly until just barely boiling. Add vanilla. Pour over your favorite ice cream and enjoy!

**Restaurant Recipe**

## Old-Fashioned Root Beer Float

**⅓ cup high quality root beer syrup**

**⅔ cup carbonated water**

**2 scoops premium vanilla ice cream**

Add root beer syrup and carbonated water to a frozen mug; stir. Slowly roll 2 round scoops of ice cream into mug. Do not stir. (This may be made in a drinking glass, but it is better in the frozen mug.)

**Restaurant Recipe**

# Leona General Store and Steakhouse

**136 North Leona Boulevard**
**Leona, TX 75850**
**903-344-2202**
**www.leonageneralstore.com**

The Leona General Store was transformed from a general store/gas station into a steakhouse in 1998. It has been expanded 5 times, and serves an average of more than 600 customers on Friday and Saturday nights. The population of Leona is only 181. Customers come from many cities and towns in Texas, as well as foreign countries as they visit family and friends in the area. It has become a meeting place for people traveling between Houston and Dallas. Most customers claim to have eaten the best steaks ever at the Leona General Store.

**Thursday: 5:30 pm to 8:30 pm**
**Friday & Saturday: 5:30 pm to 9:00 pm**

## Oatmeal Chocolate Chip Cookie

1 cup butter-flavored Crisco

1 cup brown sugar

1 cup white sugar

2 eggs

3 tablespoons vanilla

1½ to 2 cups all-purpose flour (more for cake-like cookie)

1 teaspoon salt

1 teaspoon baking soda

3 cups oatmeal

1 (10-ounce) package bittersweet chocolate (Ghirardelli 60% Cacoa Premium Baking Chips)

Cream together Crisco, brown sugar and white sugar. Add eggs and vanilla; blend until smooth. In a separate bowl, mix flour, salt and baking soda. Slowly add to Crisco and egg mixture. Mix until smooth. Fold in oatmeal, 1 cup at a time. Add baking chips; stir. Form by hand into palm-size cookies. Bake at 350° for 12 minutes.

**Family Favorite**

## Jalapeño Yeast Roll Soufflé

10 (1-inch) cubes Leona General Store yeast rolls

1½ cups sharp Cheddar or jalapeño Jack cheese

¾ cup sliced jalapeños

1 cup cubed Leona General Store steak, ham or sausage (optional)

1 (8-ounce) package cream cheese, softened

8 large eggs

1½ cups milk

⅔ cup half-and-half

Salt and pepper to taste

Leona General Store spice mix

Place half of the yeast roll cubes in a 9x13-inch baking dish coated with cooking spray. Layer 1 cup cheese, jalapeños and steak over rolls. Beat cream cheese at medium speed of mixer until smooth. Add eggs, 1 at a time, mixing well after each addition. Add milk, half-and-half, salt and pepper. Pour half of mixture over pan. Place remaining yeast roll cubes on top and pour remaining egg mixture over rolls. Cover and refrigerate overnight. Remove bread mixture from refrigerator. Sprinkle top with Leona General Store spice; let stand on counter for 30 minutes. Bake at 375° for 50 minutes or until set. Sprinkle soufflé with remaining ½ cup cheese 10 minutes before baking completed.

**Family Favorite**

# Ann's Seafood

**725 Main Street
Liberty, TX 77575
936-334-0306**

If you are looking for the best seafood around and that feeling of home, you can't go wrong with Ann's Seafood. With a wide variety of items to choose from, if you can't find something to eat, you're just not hungry. From the jumbo shrimp platter to the homemade mashed

potatoes and coleslaw you can't go wrong. You will be greeted by a friendly wait staff who are there to please you and make sure your visit is top of the line. The only mistake you can make is not saving room for a piece of homemade pie. There is plenty of room for those large parties. See you there.

**Monday – Saturday: 11:00 am to 9:00 pm**

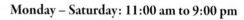

## Crawfish Ètouffée

1 stick real butter
1 bunch green onions, chopped
1 or 2 bell peppers, chopped
1 (23-ounce) can cream of
mushroom soup
1 (1-pound) package crawfish tails
2 tablespoons Tony Chachere's
Creole seasoning
2 tablespoons black pepper

Melt butter in large pan. Add onion and bell pepper. Simmer until wilted. Add soup and heat through, slowly stirring often. Add crawfish; cover and heat through, slowly stirring often. Don't overcook; if you do, crawfish will toughen. Season with Creole seasoning and black pepper (use more or less to suit your taste). Serve over white rice with hot sauce on the side. This dish is even better the next day.

**Restaurant Recipe**

## Fried Alligator Tail

1 pound alligator tail, cut into chunks
2 tablespoons Tony Chachere's
Creole seasoning
2 tablespoons Old Bay Seasoning
1 egg, beaten
2 cups buttermilk
1 cup all-purpose flour

Season meat with Tony Chachere's and Old Bay seasonings. Mix egg and buttermilk together until blended. Pour over meat and refrigerate overnight. Buttermilk mixture should cover meat (if not, add additional buttermilk). When ready to cook, remove meat from buttermilk (do not rinse) and lightly dredge in flour. Fry in hot oil just until cooked through, about 2 minutes. (Do not overcook. Gator will get tough if you cook it too long.)

**Restaurant Recipe**

# River City Grille

**700 1st Street**
**Marble Falls, TX 78654**
**830-798-9909**
**www.rivercitygrilletx.com**

At River City Grille, the best family traditions start in the kitchen. The extensive menu features favorites like chicken-fried steak, burgers, Hill Country famous pork chops, and a variety of unique selections created from family recipes. All of the dressings, sides, and desserts are homemade. Steaks are hand-cut from Certified Angus Beef. Dine inside surrounded by rustic, Texas lake décor or relax on one of the decks overlooking Lake Marble Falls. There is a full-service bar stocked with spirits, local beers, and a variety of wines. The friendly staff makes River City Grille a Highland Lakes favorite.

**Monday – Saturday: 11:00 am to 10:00 pm**
**Sunday: 11:00 am to 9:00 pm**

## Spinach Dip

1 ounce (2 tablespoons) butter

2 tablespoons vegetable oil

1½ cups diced onions

1 teaspoon minced garlic

2 tablespoons flour

½ cup chicken broth

½ cup whipping cream

1 cup grated Parmesan cheese

½ cup shredded Cheddar cheese

½ cup shredded Jack cheese

½ cup sour cream

¾ pound frozen spinach, thawed, chopped and drained

⅛ teaspoon cayenne pepper

½ teaspoon salt

Melt butter with oil in a stockpot over medium heat. Add onions and garlic; sauté until onions are wilted. Add flour and stir continually for 2 minutes. Slowly add chicken broth and whipping cream; bring to a slight boil and continue to cook until mixture begins to thicken. Remove from heat; stir in cheeses, sour cream, spinach, cayenne pepper and salt. Mix well. Refrigerate until ready to use. Makes 1 quart.

Preheat oven to 350°. Place in baking dish; bake 12 to 15 minutes or until top browns. Remove from oven and serve with toasted baguettes or tortilla chips.

**Restaurant Recipe**

## Connie's Chocolate Cake

2 cups all-purpose flour

2 cups sugar

4 tablespoons cocoa

1 cup water

2 sticks butter

2 eggs

½ cup buttermilk

1 teaspoon each: baking soda, cinnamon and vanilla extract

Preheat oven to 400°. Grease 9x13-inch pan. Combine flour and sugar and set aside. In saucepan, combine cocoa, water and butter. Bring to a rolling boil over medium heat. Add flour mixture and mix well. Lower heat and continue to cook about 5 minutes. Add eggs, buttermilk, baking soda, cinnamon and vanilla. Mix well and pour into pan. (Batter will be runny.) Bake 25 minutes. Cool before icing.

### Icing:

1 stick butter

⅓ cup whole milk

4 tablespoons cocoa

1 cup chopped Texas pecans

1 (16-ounce) package powdered sugar

Combine butter, milk, cocoa and pecans in a saucepan over medium heat. Stir and cook until well combined. Add powdered sugar; mix well. Pour over cooled cake. Serve warm with vanilla ice cream.

**Restaurant Recipe**

# Donald Citrano's
# Coffee Shop Cafe

**1005 West McGregor Drive**
**McGregor, TX 76657**
**254-840-2027**
www.thecoffeeshop.us
www.facebook.com/thecoffeeshopcafe
www.pieladylife.com

The Coffee Shop Café, owned and operated by long time restaurateur Donald Citrano, is located just outside Waco on Highway 84. When you're hankering for some real home cooking, this place is a must. Southern fried catfish, chicken-fried steak, the best burgers, hand-battered onion rings, and made-from-scratch pies are some of the reasons that they

have been featured in *Texas Monthly Magazine* and *Southern Living's Second Helpings Cookbook*. Choose from the daily buffet and salad bar, or order from their extensive menu. Breakfast is served all day, and their famous breakfast buffet is served on weekend mornings. Whatever you choose, be sure to save room for Valerie's homemade pie!

**Monday – Saturday: 6:00 am to 9:00 pm**
**Sunday: 6:00 am to 2:00 pm**

## Dr. Pepper Cake

*Wacoans have been drinking Dr. Pepper since Charles Alderton invented his concoction in 1885 in Waco's Old Corner Drug Store. You may be lucky enough to visit the Coffee Shop Cafe on one of the special days Valerie makes this fudgy cake as our complimentary dessert of the day with your entrée.*

2 cups all-purpose flour, sifted with
2 cups sugar
1½ cups miniature marshmallows
½ cup butter
½ cup Crisco
3 tablespoons cocoa
1 cup Dr. Pepper (or cola)
1½ cups buttermilk
1 teaspoon baking soda
2 eggs, beaten

Add marshmallows to flour mixture. In saucepan, boil butter, Crisco, cocoa and Dr. Pepper, stirring constantly. (Do not scorch.) Add to flour mixture. Beat in buttermilk, baking soda and eggs. Pour into greased and floured Bundt pan. Bake 45 minutes at 350°.

### Cola Icing:

½ cup butter
3 tablespoons cocoa
6 tablespoons Dr. Pepper (or cola)
4 cups powder sugar, sifted
1 cup chopped pecans

Boil butter, cocoa and Dr. Pepper in medium saucepan, stirring constantly. Add to powdered sugar. Stir in pecans. Pour over warm cake.

**Restaurant Recipe**

## Sweet Potato Jalapeño Soup

½ pound bacon, cut in ¼-inch strips
½ large yellow onion, finely chopped
2 cloves fresh garlic, finely minced
3 pounds sweet potatoes, peeled and cut into chunks
1 (1-quart) box chicken broth
1 teaspoon salt
½ tablespoon ground cumin
¼ cup chopped pickled jalapeños
1 teaspoon black pepper
½ cup finely chopped (stems removed) fresh cilantro
1 cup half-and-half

In large pot over medium heat, fry bacon till almost crisp. Using a slotted spoon, remove bacon and drain on paper towel. Add onion to bacon grease in pot and sauté until translucent; do not brown. Add garlic and cook a minute more. Add sweet potatoes, chicken broth, salt and cumin; bring to a boil. Lower heat to medium low, cover pot and simmer till sweet potatoes are tender. Carefully transfer half the hot mixture to a blender (or use a large metal bowl with an immersion blender). Use hand potato masher to crush up sweet potatoes still in pot. Add blended mixture back to pot on stove. Add pepper, cilantro and half-and-half and simmer another 20 minutes. Serve in bowls topped with a bacon crumbles and jalapeño cornbread on the side.

**Restaurant Recipe**

# Farm House Restaurant

**1401 East Milam Street**
**Mexia, TX 76667**
**254-472-0512**
**www.farm-house-restaurant.com**

Imagine a place where you walk in greeted with people smiling, seeing familiar faces and old friends inviting you to sit with them, a place where you catch up with people you know, with great looking plates of food filling up the restaurant, antiques and beautiful animal mounts blending in with the smell of great food being grilled and fried to perfection. This is what walking into the Farm House Restaurant is like. If you're seeking some of the best fried catfish, fried pickles, steaks, chicken-fried steak, and other southern classics, then this is the place—where the food is always cooked the same no matter how many times you visit.

**Monday – Saturday: 11:00 am to 9:00 pm**
**Sunday: 11:00 am to 3:00 pm**

## Onion Rings

### Breading:

*Use in preparation of onion rings, pickles, shrimp, chicken-fried steak, chicken strips and fried chicken.*

**2 (25-pound) bags bleached and enriched flour, divided**

**8 ounces garlic powder, divided**

**5 pounds Lawry's Seasoned Salt, divided**

**16 ounces MSG, divided**

Mix with clean dry hands. Dump 1 bag flour into bin. Add half the seasonings. Mix well with hands, pulling corners toward center. Add second bag flour and remaining seasonings; mix well.

### Dip:

**1½ gallons cold water**

**7 cups dry milk**

**7 cups defrosted frozen eggs**

Pour water into bucket; add dry milk and eggs. Mix well.

### Onion Ring Procedure:

Using pre-cut, refrigerated onion rings, drop a measured amount into dip. Remove, shake off excess and place into breading. Using a shaker basket, roll excess breading off onion rings and place aside at least 5 minutes prior to second breading. Put once breaded onion rings in dip and remove quickly. Bang basket removing any excess dip, pour onions in breading and lift and separate. Using shaker basket, rock and flip onion rings until breaded evenly. Heat shortening to 350°. Set timer for 2 minutes; drop onion rings in hot oil. After 45 seconds, shake to separate and cover with second fryer basket. Remove when timer goes off. Must be served hot.

**Restaurant Recipe**

## Peach Cobbler

**1 gallon peach pie filling**

**¼ cup lemon juice (real lemon)**

**2 teaspoons cinnamon**

**1 cup light brown sugar**

**1½ cups fresh milk**

**1½ cups all-purpose flour**

**4 teaspoons baking powder**

**1 teaspoon salt**

**1 cup granulated sugar**

**1 cup butter, melted**

Mix peaches, lemon juice, cinnamon and brown sugar by hand until well blended. Pour into a nongreased 18½x13-inch pan. Mix milk, flour, baking powder, salt and sugar together until smooth using a wire whip or hand mixer. Spread evenly over filling. Cover top with melted butter using a pastry brush. Bake at 325° for 45 minutes or until golden brown on top.

**Restaurant Recipe**

# Hillbillies Café

**12108 Highway 21 East
Midway, TX 75852
936-349-0333**

For down-home country cooking, visit Hillbillies Café ,where everything is fresh, nothing frozen. Everything is prepared by hand, and made with a whole lot of heart so you experience country cooking at its best—just like your mama used to make. You will love their hospitality, too, because if you want something that is on the menu, just ask, and they will do their best to accommodate you. Now that's service.

**Monday – Saturday:
6:00 am to 8:00 pm**

## *Pinto Beans*

**1 (1-pound) bag dry pinto beans
Salt and pepper to taste
3 strips bacon
1 onion, chopped**

Rinse beans; cook in a pot on high heat with water to cover. When water starts to boil, turn heat to simmer. Add remaining ingredients. Cook until beans are tender enough to smash with your thumb, 2 hours or longer.

**Restaurant Recipe**

## Homemade Chicken Strips

**1 chicken breast**

**2 eggs**

**½ cup buttermilk**

**1 cup all-purpose flour**

**Seasonings of your choice**

Cut chicken breast into strips. In a small bowl, mix eggs and buttermilk. In a separate bowl, mix flour and seasonings. Dip chicken in egg mixture then coat with flour mixture. Deep-fry at 350 ° until a nice golden brown.

**Restaurant Recipe**

## Jalapeño Wraps

**5 big jalapeño peppers, cut in half and deseeded**

**21 ounces cream cheese, softened**

**⅛ cup shredded Cheddar cheese**

**10 strips bacon, uncooked**

**Toothpicks, soaked in water**

Blanche jalapeños by dropping into boiling water then removing to ice water; drain and set aside. Combine cream cheese and Cheddar cheese. Stuff cheese mixture into jalapeños; wrap with bacon. Secure with toothpick. Place on a pit or grill at 325° and flip frequently for even cooking. Cook until bacon is crisp to your liking.

**Restaurant Recipe**

# Peggy's on the Bayou Cajun Café

**2682 East Roundbunch Road**
**Orange, TX 77630 • 409-233-7017**
**www.peggysonthebayoucajuncafe.com**

Peggy's on the Bayou Cajun Café officially opened June 2009 but has a long past. Peggy's husband of 45 years, Richard Albair, opened the seafood market in 1990, growing the business steadily. Over the years, they have survived hardships, including two hurricanes and working temporarily from a concession trailer. Today, Peggy's is well known for their eight-ounce burgers served on sweet sourdough, white, or jalapeño bread. Local favorites include seafood gumbo and boiled crawfish. Don't miss the pistolettes stuffed with seafood and Cajun nacho sauce. Longtime customers and visitors alike enjoy sitting on the back porch overlooking the bayou and watching the four-foot alligator in the water.

**Sunday: 8:00 am to 3:00 pm**
**Monday – Wednesday: 8:00 am to 8:00 pm**
**Thursday – Saturday: 8:00 am to 9:00 pm**

## Cajun Seafood Pistolettes

¾ cup butter

1 (2-pound) bag frozen seasoning blend (diced bell pepper, onion, celery and parsley)

¾ cup finely diced jalapeños

1 (28-ounce) can Rotel tomatoes

1 (10.75-ounce) can cream of mushroom soup

4 tablespoons cornstarch

2½ pounds Velveeta cheese, cubed

1 (12-ounce) bottle moscato wine

1 pound each: crawfish tails, shrimp, crabmeat

Melt butter in a large pot over medium heat. Add season blend and jalapeños; sauté until soft. Stir in Rotel, soup, cornstarch, Velveeta and wine. Increase to medium-high heat and bring to a boil. Reduce heat to medium, add shrimp and cook 5 to 7 minutes. Add crawfish and crabmeat. Turn heat to low and simmer 10 minutes, stirring occasionally.

**Restaurant Recipe**

## Shrimp and Andouille Sausage with Asiago Grits

**1 tablespoon unsalted butter**

**½ pound andouille sausage, diced**

**1½ pounds shrimp, peeled, deveined**

**¾ cup heavy cream**

**⅓ cup chicken broth**

**⅓ cup white wine**

**½ cup freshly grated Asiago cheese**

**⅓ teaspoon white pepper**

In a medium pan, melt butter over medium-high heat. Add sausage; cook, stirring, 5 minutes or until brown. Add shrimp; cook 3 to 5 minutes, stirring, till shrimp turns pink. Remove shrimp and sausage from pan. Add cream, broth and wine to pan; cook over medium heat. Stir in cheese and pepper; cook, stirring constantly, 6 to 8 minutes, or until cheese is melted. Stir in shrimp and sausage. Serve over grits.

### Asiago Grits:

**2 (14-ounce) cans chicken broth**

**¾ cup uncooked quick grits**

**½ (8-ounce) package chive and onion cream cheese**

**½ cup freshly grated Asiago cheese**

**¼ teaspoon ground white pepper**

Boil broth over medium heat; whisk in grits. Cover and reduce heat to medium-low; simmer 12 to 15 minutes or until thick, stirring occasionally. Stir in cheese and pepper until melted. Serves 6.

**Restaurant Recipe**

## Mandarin Orange Cake

**1 box yellow cake mix, plus ingredients to prepare**

**1 (15-ounce) can Mandarin orange slices**

**1 (14-ounce) can sweetened condensed milk**

**1 (15-ounce) can pineapple chunks, drained well**

**1 (5.1-ounce) box vanilla instant pudding, plus ingredients to prepare**

**1 (8-ounce) carton Cool Whip**

Mix cake batter following package directions, except replace milk with juice from Mandarin oranges. Pour into a treated 9x13-inch pan. Bake at 325° for 25 to 30 minutes or until done. Poke holes in top of cake with wooden spoon, then pour sweetened condensed milk over top. Cool completely. Drain pineapples well. Prepare pudding per package directions. Mix with Cool Whip and pineapple. Spread over cake and serve. Refrigerate leftovers.

**Restaurant Recipe**

# Big Earl's

**2999 State Highway 11 West
Pittsburg, TX 75686
903-856-3867**

Big Earl's is a family-run, Texas-veteran-owned business taking pride in their food, service, actions, and themselves. Big Earl's serves home-cooked meals like hand-battered chicken-fried steaks, half-pound hamburgers, fresh-cut French fries, catfish, shrimp, and ètouffée—everything from sandwiches to rib-eye steaks. Near Lake Bob Sandlin in the small town of Pittsburg, Big Earl's is divided into two sides—the restaurant and a bait and tackle store. You will enjoy great home cooking and can shop at the same place.

**Tuesday – Saturday: 6:00 am to 9:00 pm
Sunday: 6:00 am to 3:00 pm**

## Big Earl's Homemade Meatloaf

2½ pounds lean ground beef

2 links Italian sausage, casing removed

3 eggs

1 (5.5-ounce) can V-8 juice
(can use tomato juice)

1 (5-ounce) can evaporated milk

1 cup Italian-style breadcrumbs

1 cup chopped onion

1 cup chopped celery

¾ cup chopped red or green
bell pepper

¾ cup chopped fresh basil
(or 6 teaspoons dry basil)

1 teaspoon each: black pepper,
seasoned salt, garlic powder, and
Italian seasoning

½ cup shredded fresh Parmesan cheese
(or grated)

Heat oven to 400°. Line baking dish with foil. In large bowl, combine all ingredients. Mix well with hands. Shape in prepared pan; cover with topping.

### Topping:

½ cup ketchup

½ cup packed brown sugar

1 teaspoon ground mustard

In small bowl, whisk all ingredients together; pour over meatloaf. Bake uncovered 1 hour. Allow meatloaf to rest about 30 minutes before slicing.

**Restaurant Recipe**

## Banana Pudding

1 (5.1-ounce) package vanilla
instant pudding

2 cups cold milk

1 (14-ounce) can sweetened
condensed milk

1 tablespoon vanilla

1 (12-ounce) carton Cool Whip

1 (12-ounce) box vanilla wafers

5 to 7 bananas, sliced

Beat pudding mix and milk 2 minutes; blend in condensed milk and vanilla; fold in Cool Whip. Layer wafers, bananas (completely cover wafers), and pudding mixture. Repeat layers; chill.

**Restaurant Recipe**

## Corn Maque Choux

⅔ cup each: chopped bell pepper,
chopped onions, chopped celery

2 tablespoons minced garlic

1 stick butter

1 (28-ounce) can Rotel tomatoes

1 teaspoon minced garlic

1½ teaspoons Creole seasoning

¾ tablespoon black pepper

½ teaspoon white pepper

1 (106-ounce) can sweet corn

Dash each: thyme, basil, celery seed

Sauté bell pepper, onions, celery, and minced garlic in butter. Add remaining ingredients; cook 20 minutes until hot.

**Restaurant Recipe**

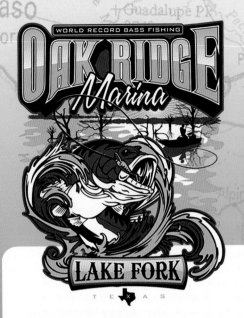

## Oak Ridge Marina, Motel & Restaurant

**2919 West State Highway 154 • Quitman, TX 75783**
**903-878-2529 • www.oakridgemarina.com**

For the best, unobstructed view of Lake Fork come to Oak Ridge Marina. Have a hearty breakfast before hitting the lake, and come back for a great lunch of burgers, catfish, or the daily special. Local favorites include the smoked ribs cooked low and slow and pulled pork cooked onsite in the house smoker. Relax to a stunning view of the sunset on the water while eating a choice-cut rib-eye, New York strip or sirloin steak with the best salad bar within 25 miles. Saturday Special is the popular

Prime Rib, which sells out quickly, so be sure to dine early. For great food with an unforgettable view, and even the option to stay overnight, visit Oak Ridge Marina.

**SPRING HOURS:**
Monday – Thursday: 5:30 am to 8:00 pm
Friday & Saturday: 5:30 am to 9:00 pm
Sunday: 5:30 am to 3:00 pm

## East Texas Cowboy Soup

*We have taken our three-hour soup recipe and condensed it down to a half hour preparation for you busy cooks at home.*

**2 tablespoons butter**

**1 cup diced onions**

**1 pound hamburger meat**

**4 potatoes, baked, cooled, peeled and cut into 1-inch pieces**

**1 (10-ounce) can Rotel tomatoes**

**1 (15-ounce) can pinto beans**

**1 (28-ounce) can minestrone soup (ready to eat; not condensed)**

**Shredded cheese for topping**

In a large pot, melt butter over medium heat; add onions and cook until soft. Add hamburger meat and cook, stirring often to break into small pieces, until brown; drain. Add potato pieces and mix thoroughly. Add tomatoes and pinto beans; mix well. Add soup and bring to a soft boil for a few minutes. (Tip: If you prefer a thinner soup, add chicken stock.) Top individual servings with cheese and serve with cornbread or dinner roll.

**Restaurant Recipe**

## Texas Onion Rings

*Everything's bigger in Texas—even our onion rings.*

**1 quart buttermilk**

**2 jumbo eggs**

**5 cups all-purpose flour**

**1 tablespoon garlic powder**

**1½ teaspoons Season-All**

**1½ teaspoons ground pepper**

**2¼ teaspoons salt**

**3 super colossal onions (over 4-inch diameter)**

**4 cups vegetable oil**

Mix buttermilk and eggs in large bowl. Sift together flour, garlic powder, Season-All, pepper and salt in a separate large bowl. Wash and peel skin from onions, slicing off ends. Slice onions in 1-inch to 1¼-inch width, making "rings." Pull rings apart keeping the largest for onion rings. (Save the small pieces to chop up for Cowboy Soup.) Heat vegetable oil in deep fryer or in deep pan on stovetop to 350°. One at a time, dip rings in milk mixture, then in flour mixture, coating entire ring. Repeat, dipping twice in milk and twice in flour. Shake off excess flour mixture before frying. Using tongs, carefully place breaded onion rings into hot oil cooking a few rings at a time. Carefully turn each ring once to ensure both sides are cooked to a golden brown (about 3 minutes each side). Drain on paper towels. Serve with ranch dressing for a great side dish or appetizer.

**Restaurant Recipe**

# The Fatted Calf

**112 East Rusk Street • Rockwell, TX 75087**

**972-722-3343**

**www.thefattedcalfrestaurant.com**

The Fatted Calf, on the square in downtown Rockwell, specializes in "down home chic" food at a reasonable price. It is a comfortable, upscale restaurant serving breakfast, lunch, and dinner, Tuesday through Sunday. Special dinners and evening events take place throughout the year. Daily specials are offered, and feature only the freshest, seasonal ingredients. Chef Ted Grieb was raised by his mother (a great cook) and father (a great fisherman) in southern New Jersey where he developed a love for farm fresh food, freshly caught seafood, and large portions. He brings that talent to The Fatted Calf.

**Tuesday – Sunday: 7:30 am to 2:00 pm; 5:00 pm to 9:30 pm**
**Friday & Saturday: Open until 10:30 pm**

## Egg Custard Casserole

**3 cups milk**

**4 tablespoons butter**

**1½ cups sugar**

**Pinch salt**

**6 eggs, beaten**

**1 tablespoon vanilla**

Scald milk, butter, sugar and salt in a saucepan. Add a small amount of milk mixture to beaten eggs to temper. Then add eggs to milk mixture, stirring constantly, until well mixed. Add vanilla and mix. Pour mixture into buttered round casserole dish. Cook at 450° for 10 minutes. Turn down heat to 350° and cook 10 more minutes or until knife inserted in middle comes out clean.

**Local Favorite**

## Bourbon Balls

**3 cups crushed vanilla wafers**

**3 tablespoons white corn syrup**

**1 cup powdered sugar**

**½ cup cocoa**

**1 cup chopped pecans**

**½ cup bourbon**

In a bowl, mix all ingredients together and form into small balls. Roll balls in your choice of covering: powdered sugar, cocoa, melted chocolate, nuts or coconut. They are all good.

**Local Favorite**

## Orange Pork Chops

**6 pork chops**

**1 cup orange juice**

**1 teaspoon salt**

**¼ teaspoon black pepper**

**½ teaspoon dry mustard**

**¼ cup brown sugar**

Place chops in roasting pan. Mix other ingredients and pour on top. Bake at 350° for 1 hour, basting every 15 minutes.

**Local Favorite**

# Another Time Soda Fountain & Café

**800 Third Street
Rosenberg, TX 77471
281-232-2999
www.anothertimesodafountain.com**

Another Time Soda Fountain & Café, in a renovated 1900's building, is not your ordinary café. When you step into the café, you immediately are transformed back to a simpler time. They have daily blue plate specials, but come early they go fast, and daily homemade soups. Meat is purchased from a local meat market daily. Try a half-pound burger or chicken-fried steak fingers. The ice cream sodas and malts are as authentic as if you were back in the 50's, and don't forget the fountain drinks made by soda jerks. Try the one-pound banana splits made with Blue Bell ice cream. Delicious.

**Wednesday – Sunday: 11:00 am to 5:00 pm
Friday & Saturday: Open until 8:00 pm**

## Banana Layer Cake

2 cups all-purpose flour
1 teaspoon baking soda
1 teaspoon baking powder
½ teaspoon salt
1½ cups sugar
1 cup shortening
2 eggs, well beaten
¾ cup buttermilk
1 cup mashed bananas
1 teaspoon vanilla

Sift flour, baking soda, baking powder and salt. Beat sugar and shortening until fluffy. Add eggs; beat well. Add flour mixture alternately with buttermilk. Mix in bananas and vanilla. Bake in 2 layers at 375° for 25 minutes or until done. Cool.

### *White Mountain Frosting:*

½ cup sugar
2 tablespoons water
¼ cup light corn syrup
2 egg whites
2 tablespoons powdered sugar
1 teaspoon vanilla

In saucepan, bring sugar, water and corn syrup to rolling boil. Boil rapidly without stirring to 242° on candy thermometer. Beat egg whites with powdered sugar until stiff peaks form. Pour hot sugar in thin stream into egg whites, beating constantly on medium speed then on high until stiff peaks form. Add vanilla during last minute of beating. Frost cake.

**Restaurant Recipe**

## Smothered Pork Steaks

10 pork steaks
Salt
Pepper
Garlic powder

Season pork steaks with salt, pepper and garlic powder to taste. Bake at 325° for 30 minutes. While baking, make gravy.

### *Gravy:*

Sliced onions
1 stick butter
¼ cup all-purpose flour
1 quart beef broth
Salt and pepper to taste

Sauté onions and butter in skillet. Remove onions; add flour and brown. Add broth, onions, salt and pepper. Simmer 5 minutes; pour over baked pork steaks; return to oven 20 minutes. Serve with German potatoes and sauerkraut.

**Restaurant Recipe**

# Old Fashioned Burgers & Ice Cream

**882 North Main Street**
**Salado, TX 76571**
**254-947-5271**
**www.facebook.com/burgersICEcream**

The name of this restaurant says it all—Old Fashioned Burgers & Ice Cream is exactly what you get at this outstanding restaurant. They use only fresh—never frozen—100% all-beef patties, which are always cooked to order and served on a lightly buttered, special bun with a side of old-fashioned fries. The milkshakes, too, are made the old-fashioned way—hand-dipped and made with real ice cream. Even the service is old-fashioned, as you'll find everyone super friendly and ready to serve. If you are in Salado, don't miss Old Fashioned Burgers & Ice Cream.

**Sunday – Thursday:**
**11:00 am to 7:00 pm**
**Friday & Saturday:**
**11:00 am to 9:00 pm**

## Dirty South Burger

**1 certified Angus beef patty**

**All-Seasoning spice
(2 sprinkles each side)**

**1 (1-ounce) slice Cheddar cheese**

**1 Kaiser bun**

**3 slices bacon, cooked**

**2 tablespoons mayonnaise**

**1 lettuce leaf**

**2 (¼-inch thick) tomato slices**

**1 fried egg**

Sprinkle seasoning mix on 1 side of burger; cook on grill at 325° until blood appears on surface. Turn burger; sprinkle with seasoning mix. Cook until blood appears on surface. Place Cheddar cheese on burger; melt with metal lid over top. Crisscross bacon slices over melted cheese. Toast bun at 200°. Place hot burger on bottom half of bun. Top with lettuce, tomato and fried egg. Spread mayonnaise on top half of bun. Close burger presentation with bun top.

**Restaurant Recipe**

## Salado Legend Burger

**1 certified Angus beef patty**

**All-Seasoning spice**

**Barbecue sauce**

**1 Kaiser bun, toasted**

**2 (½-ounce) slices Cheddar cheese**

**3 slices applewood bacon, cooked**

**1 lettuce leaf**

**1 tomato slice, ¼-inch thick**

**3 dill pickle slices**

**2 (¼-inch thick) red onion slices,
separated into rings**

**2 ounces fries**

Sprinkle seasoning mix on 1 side of burger; cook on grill at 325° until the blood appears on the surface. Turn burger and sprinkle other side with seasoning mix; cook until the blood appears on the surface (this is medium) or to desired doneness. Baste burger with barbecue sauce 1 minute prior to removing from grill. Place Cheddar cheese on burger; melt with metal lid cover. Toast buns at 200°. Place hot burger on bottom half of bun. Top with bacon, lettuce, tomato, pickles, and onion rings in that order. Close burger presentation with the bun top; lay fries on the side.

**Restaurant Recipe**

# Ecclectiques

**208 West Duval Street**
**Troup, TX 75789**
**903-842-5001**
www.facebook.com/pages/Ecclectiques

Ecclectiques is an antique and gift shop located in the small east Texas town of Troup, featuring a bistro that serves delicious home cooking. Owner, René Stovall, and her two best friends, Donna Dowdy and Pam Kidd, all born and raised in Troup, are proud to have the opportunity to excel in what they love. Ecclectiques provides patrons a place to sit back, relax and enjoy a homemade meal over the infamous small town talk and the prospect of finding a diamond in the rough, whether it be old or new.

**Tuesday – Friday: 10:00 am to 5:30 pm**
**Saturday: 10:00 am to 2:00 pm**

## Cornbread Salad

1 pan prepared cornbread
1 cup chopped chives
1 cup diced tomatoes
15 ounces fresh corn
1 pound bacon, cooked until crisp and crumbled
1 cup mayonnaise
1 (1-ounce) package dry ranch dressing mix

Crumble cooled cornbread into a large bowl. Add chives, tomatoes, corn and bacon; stir until evenly mixed. In a separate bowl, combine mayo and ranch dressing mix. Add mayonnaise mixture to salad and stir until evenly mixed. Cover and refrigerate at least 2 hours. Serve with a garnish of sliced fresh cherry tomatoes.

**Restaurant Recipe**

## Pam's Corn and Crab Bisque

½ cup finely chopped white onion

1 stick butter

64 ounces homemade chicken broth
with chicken bouillon

5 (6-ounce) cans lump white crabmeat

4 ears fresh corn, cut off of the cob

2 cups heavy cream

Salt to taste

White pepper to taste

Fresh parsley, for garnish

In a stockpot, sauté onion in butter until translucent (but not brown). Add broth and bring to a boil. Once boiling, add crab (with juice) and corn. Reduce heat to low and simmer 20 minutes. Remove from heat and slowly stir in cream. Add salt and white pepper to taste. Serve with a garnish of fresh parsley.

**Restaurant Recipe**

## Fresh Peach Pie

### Crust:

1½ cups all-purpose flour

1½ sticks cold butter

1 cup chopped nuts

Cut butter into flour with a fork; add nuts. Press into bottom of lightly greased 9x13-inch pan. Bake at 375° for 15 minutes. Cool before filling.

### Filling:

1 (8-ounce) package cream cheese, softened

½ cup sugar

1 (8-ounce) carton Cool Whip, divided

2 cups water

2 cups sugar

6 tablespoons cornstarch

1 (3-ounce) package peach Jell-O

6 to 8 fresh peaches, peeled and sliced

Combine cream cheese, sugar and ½ cup Cool Whip; mix well and spread on cooled crust. Combine water, sugar and cornstarch in a small saucepan. Cook over medium-high heat until mixture begins to thicken. Add Jell-O and mix well. Set aside to cool. When cool, add peaches. Pour into crust and refrigerate. Before serving top with remaining Cool Whip (or freshly whipped cream).

**Restaurant Recipe**

# Kiepersol

**3933 FM 344 East • Tyler, TX 75703**
**903-894-3300 • www.kiepersol.com**

The back roads of east Texas create the perfect niche for a wine, food and spirits destination. Just south of Tyler, Kiepersol makes you welcome whether you are looking for an unparalleled steak experience, award-winning Texas wines grown on the estate or a distilled adventure touring the behind-the-scenes making of bourbon, vodka and rum. Restless souls find peace overnighting at the luxurious bed and breakfast, fulfilled by a gourmet breakfast and walking through the beautiful wooded estates. Timeless and beautiful, this hidden gem is one to remember.

**Tuesday – Friday: 11:00 am to 10:00 pm**
**Saturday: 7:00 am to 10:00 pm**

## Dirk's Dirty "Tini"

**3 ounces Dirk's Texas Vodka**

**2 ounces olive juice**

Mix well. Served chilled straight up in a martini glass garnished with homemade blue cheese and jalapeño stuffed olives.

**Restaurant Recipe**

## Dirk's Strawberry-Basil Cooler

**1½ ounces Dirk's Texas Vodka**

**2 strawberries, muddled**

**1 large basil leaf, muddled**

**½ ounce simple syrup**

**1 ounce fresh-squeezed lime juice**

**2 ounces club soda**

Mix well. Serve on the rocks garnished with a lime slice.

**Restaurant Recipe**

## Pierre's Tropical Rum Punch

**1½ ounces Pierre's Texas Rum**

**½ ounce grenadine**

**1½ ounces passion fruit syrup**

**1 ounce pineapple juice**

**2 ounces guava nectar**

Mix well. Serve on the rocks garnished with an orange slice and a cherry.

**Restaurant Recipe**

## Texas Sunset

**1½ ounces Jimmy's Texas Bourbon**

**1½ ounces pink grapefruit juice**

**1½ ounces lemonade**

**½ ounce cranberry juice**

Mix well. Serve on the rocks garnished with a lemon wheel.

**Restaurant Recipe**

## The Co-Pilot

**2 ounces Jimmy's Texas Bourbon**

**½ ounce fresh-squeezed lemon juice**

**1 ounce triple sec**

**½ ounce orgeat syrup**

Mix well. Serve on the rocks garnished with an orange twist.

**Restaurant Recipe**

# The Stand

**16700 FM 2493, Suite 1600**
**Tyler, TX 75703**
**903-574-9603**
**www.thestandhotdogs.com**
**Find us on Facebook:**
**Fans of the Stand**

The Stand Hot Dogs & Sausages infuses all the mouthwatering tastes of a big city hot dog joint into a small, one-red-light community. Offering culinary creativity, cleanliness, southern hospitality, and the character of a historic east Texas building, The Stand is a local favorite and destination restaurant for those traveling east Texas. Enjoy a variety of dogs and sausages where a seat is often hard to find—friends and strangers alike often squeeze in to share the same picnic table. Or, enjoy a breakfast taco and a cup of coffee for breakfast with friends. The Stand has been named one of the best restaurants in the Tyler area.

**Monday – Friday: 6:00 am to 7:00 pm**
**Saturday: 7:00 am to 7:00 pm**

## Hawaiian Hot Dogs with Mango Salsa

### Mango Salsa:

**1 large ripe mango, peeled and diced**

**½ small red onion, diced**

**1 small red bell pepper, seeded and diced**

**¼ cup chopped cilantro**

**1 serrano chile, seeded and minced**

**1 tablespoon olive oil**

**Salt and pepper to taste**

Toss together all salsa ingredients; set aside.

### Pineapple Mustard:

**⅔ cup chopped fresh pineapple**

**1 small garlic clove**

**½ cup Dijon mustard**

**1 tablespoon honey**

In a food processor, purée pineapple, garlic, mustard and honey until smooth.

### Hot Dogs:

**8 hot dogs**

**8 hot dog buns**

**2 ripe avocados, sliced**

Preheat grill to high heat. Open buns and grill face-down 1 minute until golden brown. Grill hot dogs until internal temperature reaches 165°. Place hot dogs on buns and top with mango salsa, pineapple mustard and avocado.

**Family Favorite**

## Cheesy Garlic Bombs

**¼ cup unsalted butter, melted**

**3 cloves garlic, minced**

**½ teaspoon dried oregano**

**½ teaspoon dried basil**

**¼ teaspoon salt**

**1 (8-ounce) can crescent rolls**

**48 mozzarella pearls, drained**

**¼ cup freshly grated Parmesan cheese**

**2 tablespoons chopped fresh parsley leaves**

Preheat oven to 375°. Lightly oil a 24-cup mini muffin pan. In a small bowl, whisk together butter, garlic, oregano, basil and salt; set aside. Half each crescent roll, making 16 pieces. Add 3 mozzarella pearls to the center of each crescent piece and roll into a ball. Place into prepared muffin tin. Brush butter mixture over rolls and bake until golden brown. Sprinkle with Parmesan and parsley.

**Family Favorite**

# Lula Jane's

**406 Elm Avenue • Waco, TX 76704**
**254-366-0862 • www.lulajanes.com**

Situated in a redeveloping area of Waco, Lula Jane's became Waco's first "garden to table" bakery restaurant. Everything served is made from scratch by an incredible chef and bakery staff. The environment is flushed with natural light—perfect for gathering folks inside or on the porches to enjoy the best baked goods in the area. They also serve a few breakfast meals and a daily farm-fresh lunch special. The bread loaves, pies, and cakes are beyond compare, and the chocolate chip cookies are famous with the locals. Let the friendly staff help make you happy with "Good Food and Good Folk."

**Monday: 9:00 am to 3:00 pm**
**Tuesday – Friday: 7:30 am to 3:00 pm**
**Saturday: 8:00 am to 3:00 pm**

GOOD FOLKS · LULA JANES · GOOD FOOD

## LJ's Breakfast Pie

1 deep-dish pie shell, baked

2 cups hash browns, browned
(10 minutes in oven)

1 cup browned sausage or cooked and
chopped bacon (optional)

1 cup shredded Cheddar cheese,
plus a little more for topping

4 eggs

¾ cup milk or ½ cup milk plus
¼ cup half-n-half

1 teaspoon salt

¼ teaspoon pepper

Dash nutmeg

1 tablespoon sugar

1 tablespoon flour

½ (4-ounce) can green chiles

2 heaping tablespoons cooked
chopped onion

In prebaked pie shell, layer potatoes on bottom. Top with precooked meat (if including) then 1 cup cheese. Whisk remaining ingredients and pour over top. Top with additional cheese. Bake 42 minutes at 350° in convection oven (longer if not using convection).

**Restaurant Recipe**

## Lula Jane's Iced Tea Recipe

*Our tea is a blend that folks so love on a hot day. It is an often requested recipe; this is the first time we have shared it.*

4 black tea bags

1 fruit tea bag
(example: raspberry hibiscus)

1 mint tea bag

4 cups boiling water

Run a hot water brew and steep all tea bags about 4 to 6 minutes. Remove tea bags, add ice and water to desired strength. Refrigerate before serving. Enjoy!

**Restaurant Recipe**

# Texas
# Great Country Cafe
# & Pie Pantry

**903 South Bosque**
**Waco, TX 76692**
**254-694-3608**
**www.texasgreatcountrycafe.com**

Owner/operators Judy and Chrystal, a mother/daughter duo working together since 1996, opened their Whitney location in 2009. From the moment you walk in, it's easy to see they are all about Texas, doing their best to satisfy whatever hankerin' you might have with great food, including hand-breaded chicken-fried steak, hearty breakfasts served all day, plenty of tasty salads and "sammiches," plus a variety of homemade pies, cheesecakes, and cakes made daily in the in-house bakery. The down-home music, comfy surroundings, and true hospitality make the perfect setting for enjoying family and friends.

**Monday – Saturday: 7:00 am to 9:00 pm**
**Sunday: 7:00 am to 3:00 pm**

## Chicken Spaghetti

1 small onion, chopped

2 stalks celery, finely sliced

1 tablespoon butter

6 ounces spaghetti, cooked
and drained

1 chicken, boiled and deboned

1 (10.75-ounce) can cream of
chicken soup

1 (8-ounce) can mushrooms, drained

1 (2.25-ounce) can sliced black olives,
drained

½ to 1 (4-ounce) can green chiles,
chopped

1 (4-ounce) jar pimentos

Salt and pepper to taste

Cheddar cheese, desired amount

Sauté onion and celery in butter until crisp/tender. Mix together with spaghetti, chicken, and remaining ingredients, except cheese. Pour into baking dish coated with nonstick cooking spray. Heat in 350° oven until slightly bubbly. Top with cheese and continue to heat until cheese is melted.

**Restaurant Recipe**

## Pecan Pie

1 cup sugar

2 tablespoons flour

3 eggs, slightly beaten

1 cup light Karo syrup

2 tablespoons melted butter

1 teaspoon vanilla

1 cup chopped pecans

1 (9-inch) deep-dish pie shell, unbaked

Combine sugar and flour in a mixing bowl. In a separate bowl, blend eggs, syrup, butter and vanilla. Gradually add dry ingredients to egg and butter mixture, stirring well. Sprinkle pecans over bottom of pie shell; pour liquid over pecans. Bake at 350° for 50 to 55 minutes.

**Restaurant Recipe**

# Four Winds Steakhouse

**21191 FM 47**
**Wills Point, TX 75169**
**903-873-2225**
**www.fourwindssteakhouse.com**

The Four Winds Steakhouse is elegant and rustic, perched amongst oak trees and meadows, next to a pond on a beautiful east Texas ranch. Chef Frank Rumoré and his team prepare fine steaks and seafood for their guests. The beef is aged, cut in-house daily, and cooked to order. Quality seafood is freshly prepared daily, and dressings, sauces, and desserts are house made. To compliment your dinner they have a full bar and a wine list with several boutique-style wines. It's a favorite getaway dining experience for many coming to treat themselves to excellent food and great service.

**Tuesday – Saturday:**
**5:00 pm to 10:00 pm**

## New Orleans-Style BBQ Shrimp

5 jumbo shrimp
1 lemon, divided
2 ounces whole butter
1 ounce olive oil
1 tablespoon minced garlic
6 shakes Worcestershire sauce
3 shakes Tabasco Sauce
1 teaspoon dried rosemary
⅛ teaspoon salt
⅛ teaspoon black pepper

Butterfly and devein shrimp, leaving the shell on. Place shrimp in oven-proof dish. Squeeze ½ lemon over shrimp and add remaining ingredients. Bake 8 minutes in a convection oven at 350°. Slice remaining ½ lemon and use for garnish. Serve shrimp warm with French bread. Makes 1 serving.

**Restaurant Recipe**

## Shrimp Rémoulade

2 egg yolks
¼ cup vegetable oil
½ cup minced celery
½ cup minced green onions
¼ cup chopped parsley
1 tablespoon minced garlic
1 lemon, divided
¼ cup horseradish
1 bay leaf
2 tablespoons Creole mustard
2 tablespoons ketchup
2 tablespoons Worcestershire sauce
1 tablespoon yellow mustard
1 tablespoon white vinegar
1 tablespoon Tabasco Sauce
2 teaspoons sweet paprika
1 teaspoon salt

Put egg yolks in food processor; with processor running, drizzle in oil. Add remaining ingredients and blend until all ingredients are puréed. Chill and serve with boiled shrimp. Makes 1½ cups.

**Restaurant Recipe**

# Pickett House

**157 Private Road 6000**
**Woodville, TX 75979**
**409-283-3371**
**www.heritage-village.org**

The world-famous Pickett House Restaurant serves boarding house-style all-you-can-eat fried chicken, chicken and dumplings, country vegetables, cobbler, biscuits, and cornbread with a good variety of condiments for your liking. The Pickett House still is one of the best home-style eating places in all of Texas. Folks come from all over, some even fly in by plane, to enjoy a meal here. Pickett House will open for special occasions in groups of 20 or more, with reservation. A private meeting room is available for rent.

**Monday – Friday:**
**11:00 am to 2:00 pm**

**Saturday – Sunday:**
**11:00 am to 6:00 pm**

## Peach Cobbler

**4 cups sliced fresh peaches**

**1 cup sugar**

**½ teaspoon cinnamon**

**2 tablespoons cornstarch**

**¼ cup water**

**2 tablespoons butter (or margarine)**

**1 teaspoon vanilla**

**Pie crust**

In a large heavy saucepan, combine peaches, sugar and cinnamon; boil gently 1 hour. Mix cornstarch with water until smooth. Add mixture quickly to peaches, stirring to thicken. Remove from heat; add butter and vanilla. Spray a 9x13-inch pan with cooking spray; add peaches. Top with your favorite pie crust recipe (or premade crust). Bake at 375° until crust is golden brown.

**Restaurant Recipe**

## Chicken and Dumplings

**1 whole chicken, or 4 to 5 breasts**

**2 sticks butter**

**1 tablespoon chicken bouillon granules**

**Pepper to taste**

Boil chicken in salted water to cover; debone and shred. Add butter, bouillon and pepper to broth. Set aside while broth and chicken while making dumplings.

### Dumplings:

**2 cups all-purpose flour**

**1 teaspoon salt**

**¼ cup Crisco**

**4 eggs**

In a bowl, add flour, salt and Crisco; mix until crumbly. Add eggs to 1 cup water and mix well. Pour slowly into flour mixture; mix together. (Dough should be sticky; if dry, add more water.) Place dough on a floured board; roll out small amounts at a time until very thin. Cut into strips then squares. Place chicken broth back on burner and heat to a slow boil. Drop dumplings into hot liquid; cook 15 minutes. Before serving, add shredded chicken back to broth mixture and heat through.

**Restaurant Recipe**

# Index of Restaurants

Index of Restaurants

# Index of Recipes